The Black Discovery of America

THE BLACK DISCOVERY OF AMERICA

Amazing evidence of daring voyages by ancient West African mariners

MICHAEL BRADLEY

PERSONAL LIBRARY
TORONTO

Copyright © 1981, Personal Library
ALL RIGHTS RESERVED. No part of this publication may be reproduced, stored in a retrieval system or transmitted in any form or by any means, electronic, mechanical, photocopying, recording or otherwise, without the prior written permission of the publishers.

Personal Library, Publishers
Suite 439, 17 Queen Street East
Toronto, Canada M5C 1P9

The publisher has made every effort to give accurate credit to the sources of quotations and illustrations which appear in this book. In the event of error or omission, notification would be appreciated.

Canadian Cataloguing in Publication Data

Bradley, Michael, 1944–
 The Black discovery of America

ISBN 0-920510-36-1

1. America - Discovery and exploration - West African. 2. America - Discovery and exploration - Pre-Columbian. I. Title.

E109.A35B73   970.01'1   C81-094206-2

Publisher: Glenn Edward Witmer
Editor: Ex Libris
Production Editor: Mark Eric Miller
Design: Anodos/Pamela Patrick
Composition: Video Text Inc./Rupert Bisram

Distributed to the trade by
John Wiley and Sons Canada Limited
22 Worcester Road
Rexdale, Ontario M9W 1L1

Printed and bound in Canada
by T. H. Best Printing Company Limited

For Jason

**Africa was but the glass wherein darkly I learnt to find
Vision of your face and reflect of your mind.**

Laurens van der Post

Contents

	Foreword	*xi*
	Preface	*xiv*
1.	Primitive Myths of a Savage People	*1*
2.	The Niger and the Nile	*19*
3.	The Puzzle of Diffusion	*39*
4.	Olman	*49*
5.	Green Hell?	*70*
6.	The Matter of Boats	*92*
7.	Black Ships of the Bronze Age	*120*
8.	The Evidence of Botany	*134*
9.	Possible Cultural Parallels	*140*
10.	White Gods and Lost Cities	*156*
11.	The Shared Adventure	*176*
	Notes	*183*
	Index	*190*

Foreword

Over the last twenty-five years African historians have been rebels in international academia. They have fought an almost continuous battle against the Westro-centric views of Europeans and Americans on the subject of African society and history. From early European travelers, ironically called "explorers," through European conquest and colonialism and on to the modern media and propaganda surrounding contemporary government aid programs, the image of Africa as savage, primitive, passive, chaotic and politically irresponsible has been, and is, maintained. The West insists upon seeing the world as it wishes it was, or thinks it should be. All our claims to rationality, objectivity and the scientific approach stop at the borders of our own culture. We will pay heavily for this failure on our part to extend the fairness of objectivity to other peoples and their history. Somewhere in our collective instinct we know it, and we clearly appear to prefer to melt the entire planet (or pollute it past redemption), destroying life totally, rather than become recipients of Third World charity in the form of humanitarian and psychological insights.

Academics appear to be helpless when it comes to changing our perspective. Barely effective within university walls, and ignored outside them, we are about as useful as cloistered monks within medieval monasteries when it comes to combating the historical ignorance of the surrounding population and undergraduate masses. If most academics are in the game of providing the ideology to support our short-term Western economic interest and of fostering still further our society's exclusive view of itself, all are not. Yet it seems to be true that, unfortunately, Third World studies seem to attract the most blatantly arrogant among us, those who are willing to say what Westerners want to hear and believe. When governments, publishing companies and the media turn to academia for experts on the Third World, it is too often the most arrogant and ethnocentric "experts" who are favored with advisory posts, published books or the privilege of offering the public "informed commentary" on broadcasts covering Third World events.

Few books strike so forcefully at the comfortable myths with which we surround ourselves as *The Black Discovery of America*. The truth is often illusory and complex; the truth is frequently startling as well as unwelcome. Dealing as it does with a very early period of human history, the truth presented in this book cannot be regarded as absolute, but the facts and correlations that Bradley marshals in support of his construct would seem to make the truth presented in the following pages *possible*, or even *probable*. It may confuse the reader if I remark that little more can be said of "historical truth" about events which happened only last year. The real problem in getting at "historical truth" is the nature of the assumptions that a researcher brings to his factual data. It is always comfortable to have a strong and broad foundation of fact when embarking on the presentation of a theory, but very often such a factual base only allows a writer to buttress unfounded assumptions and personal bias more convincingly, thereby appearing to be objective and thereby pretending that he has no assumptions and no bias at all.

Bradley is pugnacious in laying out his theory, and insofar as there are data concerning obscure periods of African and American history, he is responsible and accurate in his presentation of the facts. But, much more important, Bradley makes it very clear what his assumptions are, what his personal bias is. This kind of honesty is refreshing and adventurous within a culture where most writers are so damned sure they are right, within a culture where most everything is painted black or white, right or wrong, a condition that seldom or never truly exists in either society or history.

Bradley is therefore like a living and vital salmon swimming strongly against a current in an attempt to spawn new conceptions, and it is a current (or "mainstream") of historical research that is cluttered with myriads of academic dead fish whose conceptions are moribund because of too complacent acceptance of what is supposedly "right" or "wrong." He presents an interpretation of Amerindian civilization in the New World as a fusion of Amerindian and African cultures which took place long, long before Columbus. Bradley argues that the blacks not only "discovered" America before the Europeans did so but also that the blacks contributed to the rise of the high cultures which eventually emerged there.

This is a book every black person, whether African or of African descent in the diaspora, should read. Blacks in North America are preoccupied with finding a dignified place in our society and with getting their feet on a more secure rung of the economic ladder. Raising their dignity and fortifying their pride is an absolute necessity in their upward struggle for equality and mobility. There is nothing more devastating to black egos than to sit in schools year after year ingesting the myth that all worthwhile achievements and discoveries of human society originated in the white Western world, and that their ancestors were "out of it all" except as slaves recruited to tame the wilds of America. Michael Bradley's *The Black Discovery of America* provides an alternative argument to the tired fuss as to whether the Vikings (or Irish) or Columbus discovered America. This book gives blacks ammunition to shift that debate dramatically.

> Dr. James B. Webster
> Professor of African History
> Dalhousie University
> Halifax, Canada

Dr. Webster has researched in Africa and has lectured at a number of African universities—Ibadan, Makerere and the University of Malawi—from 1961 to 1972 and again from 1976 to 1979. He is the author of several books on African history and has been attached to Dalhousie University since 1972.

Preface

Several people who read *The Black Discovery of America* in manuscript form commented that it all seems obvious after the evidence for an early West African presence in the New World is presented. Invariably, even experts in African history have been led to comment along the lines of: "Why wasn't this book written twenty years ago?" Also, sooner or later, people have asked me how it was that I came upon this so obvious idea, researched the evidence and wrote this book.

The truth is that the idea wasn't mine at all, for, like most whites, I would never have thought to credit an independent African discovery of the New World (such is the strength of our prejudices). The idea was given to me by my then five-year-old son, Jason, which proves the value of a child's lack of preconceptions. It came about in this way:

One blustery March day I took Jason to McDonald's so that he could have one of those special St. Patrick's Day peppermint shakes. Looking out the window, Jason noticed an advertising billboard for Scandinavian Airlines (SAS). An airline pilot's cap rested on one horn of a traditional Viking helmet, and the slogan read: "Navigators of the world . . . since it was flat." This immediately raised a crop of five-year-old questions: "Daddy, was the world once flat?" . . . "Daddy, did people wear hats with horns a long time ago?" . . . and so on.

I launched into a rather desperate explanation of Vikings, modern Scandinavians and progressive geophysical conceptions from flat to round earth. At some point I mentioned that some people thought that Vikings first "came across the sea" to discover America. "From where?" Jason asked.

I took a napkin and tried to draw a reasonable representation of the Atlantic Ocean with the New and Old World coastlines on either side. After adding appropriate waves and a whale to the ocean, I asked Jason where he thought those Vikings had once lived.

"Well, Daddy, if they came across the ocean to discover America they must have lived here." Jason placed a sticky finger on West Africa, and went on to explain that the crossing was shortest at that place (between Brazil and West Africa) for people who only had "old time ships."

I explained that the Vikings had not come from West Africa; but after I identified Scandinavia as the Norse homeland, Jason was still unimpressed. He said that the *first* people from across the ocean to discover America must have come from West Africa because it was not far away.

This reasoning not only made a great deal of sense, but my mind immediately recalled the Olmec heads with Negroid features in Central America, and the black warriors depicted on the walls of the Temple of Warriors at Chichen Itza. I even had some vague notion that West Africa was the origin of some plants domesticated in the New World long before Columbus.

Jason's idea went around in my head for days. Ocean currents had not been drawn in on my napkin-map, but I knew that the trade-wind-driven North Equatorial Current swept from Cape Verde to the Caribbean. Not only was the Atlantic passage from West Africa to the New World shorter than the passage at other latitudes, but the winds and currents were fair and the oceanic climate gentle.

The possibility of West African voyages to America wouldn't let me alone. Finally, I spoke with my wife about this crazy idea, but first I reiterated all the old "explanations": the Olmec statues with Negroid features were of slaves brought over by the Carthagenians. That sort of thing. But the black warriors of Chichen Itza have not even had enough attention to explain them away, and it has simply been assumed that some West African plants bobbed across the Atlantic by themselves to become established in the Americas. Never mind that experts have explained that this is utterly impossible for both plantains and bottle gourds, and only barely possible for cotton. All three plants were established in the New World, not only before Columbus, but also before any record of Norse or Celtic voyages to America.

My wife, Freda, pointed out that nothing much was known about West African archeology for the very good reason that no one really cared about African history and African achievements. Anything could have happened, and much probably did—including transatlantic voyaging. "So," she shrugged, "find out."

Feeling somewhat foolish, I trekked off to the Toronto Black Peoples' Library to see what I could learn. A couple of hours reading were sufficient to discover what has been known for at least twenty years, but which has not yet found a place in our basic school histories: that the West Africans brought a proto-Egyptian civilization south of the Sahara 5,000 years ago; that the medieval civilization of Mali and other West African states could compare with the civilizations of Europe, China and India; and that it has been recorded that the emperors of Mali sent expeditions out into the Atlantic before the European Age of Discovery began.

This first discovery was later amplified considerably through correspondence with Thor Heyerdahl and Tim Severin, author of *The Brendan Voyage*, and also by the happy circumstance of meeting Professor J. B. ("Bertin") Webster of Dalhousie University's Department of African History. Through Professor Webster's efforts I was able to obtain some unpublished material pertaining to medieval Malian voyages on the Atlantic. Through his encouragement I was led to revise and rework early drafts of this book, and to prepare a paper based on the black discovery of America for the 10th Annual Conference of the Canadian Association of African Studies (held in Guelph, Ontario on May 6-9, 1980) and for the *Journal of Negro History*.

With Freda's encouragement and with Jason's active assistance I was able to prepare reed boat, balsa raft and dugout canoe models and to demonstrate that all three craft could sail to windward with the proper application of "Egyptian" (or West African) shaped paddles used as lee boards. This was an important step in proving that West Africans *could* have sailed to America and back in their huge canoes or on their reed boats . . . and an important step in my argument that the concept of the Inca *guara*, which Heyerdahl demonstrated to be efficient for windward balsa raft sailing, may have come from West Africa.

In addition, I would also like to express my thanks to Jim Phillips, president of the Dalhousie Association of Graduate Students and an avid historian, whose insight and encouragement not only helped me to persevere in completing this book, but also inspired me to plan a replica voyage from West Africa to the New World—a project that may one day be realized.

Finally, I hope that the research presented in the following pages will be judged acceptable to experts so that yet further study of possible black African influence in the New World will be undertaken by scholars; however, *The Black Discovery of America* is intended for the general reader, not the specialist. Its purpose is to modify commonly held notions of human history, and to redress historical injustice. Therefore, notes and bibliography have been combined and have been reduced to a minimum. Wherever possible, secondary and easily available sources have been referred to rather than the primary sources used.

Michael Bradley
Halifax, Canada

1

Primitive Myths of a Savage People

One December day in the year 1488, Bartholomeu Diaz stepped from the deck of his caravel onto the solid earth of Portugal and proceeded through the streets of Lisbon attended by a cheering throng of thousands. Diaz had found an end to the seemingly endless coast of Africa; he had rounded the Cape of Good Hope and had crowned Portugal's long and costly effort to find an eastern route to the Indies with undeniable success. Eastwards and north from the Cape of Good Hope lay open ocean, an ocean known to break eventually on the shores of the fabled pepper lands. Portugal's colonial fortune was made.

Perhaps not everyone in the triumphal throng cheered. There was one man among them, tall with pale blue eyes and an eagle's beak for a nose, his red hair already speckled with gray (Las Casas, Oviedo and Ferdinand all agree on this description), who, if he smiled, did so cynically. The man was Christopher Columbus, bookseller, cartographer and lately the promoter of what the experts called an impossible venture. It is written that this Italian-born adventurer "enquired into the voyages the Portuguese then made to San Jorge da Mina, and along the coast of Guinea,"[1] but his greatest fascination was for gaining knowledge of winds, currents and lands on the Atlantic. Married to the daughter of another famed Portuguese navigator, Perestrello, a discoverer of the Madeira Islands off the coast of Africa, Columbus was in possession of Perestrello's sea charts and journals.

Did Columbus smile as he turned to follow the cheering crowd and their hero Diaz because old Perestrello had unknowingly possessed a treasure in those journals and sea charts? If the coast of Africa slipping past Diaz' port beam revealed the secret of eastern navigation to the Indies, had another African cape been instrumental in unlocking an even greater mystery for Columbus?

Africa yielded to Diaz and Columbus secrets that would free Portugal and then Spain from the Middle Ages and catapult all Europe into a new era. Ironically, however, history would keep these secrets so well that even in modern time a profound darkness would remain about the true achievements of other peoples. Well-kept secrets of African capes would warp history.

It is only within the last few decades that some forgotten facts have been resurrected, that sites of ancient importance have been excavated and have laid bare what Basil Davidson has called "the Great Distortion." The truth is just now being glimpsed by a handful of specialists—it is still almost completely unsuspected by the average civilized citizen.

In the generation of Perestrello, in the years 1444 and 1445, two separate events occurred, both of immense importance to the later development of history and myth.

In 1444, the first consignment of black African slaves was landed on the quays of Lisbon. The slaves had come directly from the mouth of the Senegal River, captured and shipped by the Portuguese themselves. By the next year, the Portuguese had inched slightly farther down the African coast and had rounded Cape Verde. We will never know exactly what was written in the journals of Perestrello or what was shown on his sea charts. But Perestrello would have known mariners of this first Portuguese slaving voyage to the Senegal, and would have swapped yarns with the sailors who doubled Cape Verde. We may be sure that he shared the avidity for knowledge of all Portuguese navigators of his time and, whatever he learned, both information and rumors found safe havens in his journals and on his charts. Columbus inherited these.[2]

Frederick Pohl remarks: "We cannot see all that was in Columbus' mind, but it is obvious that when he set sail on August 3 he had some knowledge of the Atlantic Ocean that he had not publicized but that was vital to his success."[3]

Aside from the knowledge, whatever it may have been, that he inherited from Perestrello, Columbus had made a career of interviewing sailors all along the coast of Europe; and as will become clear, his work as a bookseller and cartographer was much more than just a way of making a living. It was also vital to the success of his voyage in 1492.

He began to reflect that, as the Portuguese travel so far to the southward, it were no less proper to sail away westward, and land might in reason be found that way. That he might be the more certain and confident in this particular he began to look over all the cosmographers again whom he had read before, and to observe what astronomical reasons would corroborate this project.[4]

Columbus had known with certainty that there was land to the west as early as 1477. In February and March of that year he was in the far north, in Iceland, where voyages were still being made to and from Greenland and the land beyond. Some of these voyages made in the years preceding Columbus' visit to Iceland have been recorded, while seamen who spoke with Columbus likely knew of many more.

Voyages to Greenland, and one voyage to Markland, occurred in 1362, 1372, 1380 and 1398 according to Icelandic annals, the last being made in 1408.[5] But there is little doubt that vessels sailed between Iceland, Greenland and England long after this date. On December 24, 1432, the king of England "agreed to prevent English ships from trading with dependencies of the Norwegian kingdom"[6] since the Norwegian crown had previously declared the Greenland trade a royal monopoly. English mariners, like Icelandic ones, paid scant respect to this declaration, and there was a great deal of bootleg trade by merchants of Bristol and Lynn. Hinting at this, perhaps, is the fact that a merchant guild trade factory named the Greenland Fishery still exists in Lynn and the building dates from the late 1400s.

The old Norse discovery of Greenland was definitely not forgotten in Iceland when Columbus was there in 1477. Any mariner who had sailed to Greenland would have heard about the islands and the continent that lay only 500 miles across the Davis Strait from Greenland, because most of the products exported by Greenlanders—and these products would be the reason for undertaking any voyage there—originated from the North American continent. Not only that, but the ships and boats of the Greenlanders, their roof beams and every other article of wood they possessed had come from the forests of Markland to the southwest. The Greenland Fishery itself may very well have been conducted off the Grand Banks.

But we do not have to speculate whether Columbus learned of land in the west in northern latitudes, for he tells us so himself. Pedro de Velasco of Galicia told Columbus that once when sailing for Ireland his ship "had been carried so to the northwest that they discovered land west of Ireland."[7] Another mariner, unnamed, told Columbus in Port St. Mary that "once when making a voyage to Ireland, he saw the land which he then thought to be a part of Tartary falling off toward the west, and that they could not make up to it by reason of bad weather."[8] Columbus wrote in his later years that this "presumably was the land we now call Bacalhaus [Newfoundland]."[9]

While not doubting the existence of land to the west in high northern latitudes, Columbus knew two other things as well: first, he would have learned in Iceland that the ice conditions in the Greenland seas had grown worse over the centuries and that voyages, though still made there, were becoming infrequent and hazardous. Indeed, ice conditions became so extreme by 1500 that voyages to Greenland ceased and the Greenlanders themselves perished because of the increasing harshness of their climate. The world had entered a period of climatic fluctuation, called today the Neo-boreal or "Little Ice Age."[10]

Second, Columbus was seeking the riches of the spice trade, and he knew that the northern seas and lands offered no civilized trading partners and no hope of reliable and frequent navigation by ships of his day.

But by 1484 Columbus had "concluded for certain" that lands and sea routes suiting his requirements existed. His biographer hints that Columbus' conclusion rested upon the work of cosmographers and astronomical considerations only, plus the more or less vague rumors of mariners:

> ... and therefore he took notice of what any persons whatsoever spoke to that purpose, and of sailors particularly, which might in any way be of help to him. Of all these things he made such good use that he concluded for certain that there were many lands west of the Canary Islands and Cape Verde, and that it was possible to sail and discover them.[11]

But we may rest assured that his certainty had a more concrete basis.

Cape Verde projects into the Atlantic Ocean at latitude 15 degrees north. The cape is only 1,900 miles from the coast of Brazil as the crow flies, but Atlantic winds and currents would deflect a Cape Verde mariner from this shortest route to the New World and would land his vessel not near Recife in Brazil but somewhere between the mouth of the Amazon and the entry to the Caribbean between the South American mainland and Trinidad. Cape Verde mariners had, despite the capricious deflections of trade winds and equatorial currents, much the shortest passage across the Atlantic to the regions of the New World where high cultures flourished.

Cape Verde mariners?

Cape Verde itself is flanked to the north by the Senegal River and to the south by the Gambia River. The rivers lead inland to increasingly dry country, which eventually becomes the Sahara, but they drain a coastal strip of West Africa that runs south and east around the African shore and boasts tropical African flora and fauna—and men. Cape Verde mariners, no less than the Cape Verde slaves taken by the Portuguese at the delta of the Senegal, were black Africans. And it is written that they voyaged upon the Atlantic and that these black Africans sent an expedition of "two hundred ships" into the west not two centuries before the Portuguese doubled Cape Verde. The predecessor of Emperor Kankan Musa of Mali sponsored this expedition, so it is written, and Kankan Musa himself, upon coming to power in the Empire of Mali in 1307 A.D., launched other flotillas into the far west.[12]

These expeditions must have assembled at the mouths of either the Senegal or the Gambia rivers, possibly both, and undertakings of this magnitude would not have been forgotten in the intervening years before the Portuguese arrived. For, at that time, in the time of Perestrello and the incipient slave trade, the people of the Empire of Mali wrote their own history, boasted cities as grand as any in Portugal, and as squalid. Their emperor possessed wealth beyond the imagination, but not beyond the greed, of the Portuguese themselves. And, beyond doubt, the Mali geographers possessed a knowledge of the distribution of lands and waters upon the earth more accurate than that of any European mariner of the time ... for so it is written, in the tenth chapter of Omari's *Masalik-al-absad* and in the observations of Abulfeda (1273-1332).

Columbus, a bookseller and cartographer in the exploration-obsessed society of Portuguese navigators and traders, may well have known of such accounts. And, although we may never know exactly what lay in those journals and sea charts of Perestrello, they may very well have contained memories of the descendants of mariners of Emperor Kankan Musa of Mali taken as slaves on the delta of the Senegal in 1444, or descendants of those who witnessed the assembling of the exploration fleets at the mouths of the Senegal and the Gambia.

Columbus may well have heeded what black African slaves in Portugal had to say. For, by the time Columbus acquired his certainty that land lay to the west of Cape Verde, black slaves from the region of Cape Verde had been in Portugal for forty years.

It is indeed possible, as black cultural enthusiasts assert, that Columbus shipped a black African navigator. If so, the navigator would have come from the region of Cape Verde. But it is not necessary that Columbus did so, nor is it "provable" that the navigator was, indeed, genetically black. But it is not necessary for this navigator to have been black in order to validate the claims of black Africans to the discovery of the New World. Columbus' navigator on the 1492 voyage may have been any one of several human racial representatives. If Columbus' navigator was a Moor, as has been asserted, he may well have been a black African, but may just as well have been a North African Arab, an Iberian or North African Jew (there were many such in navigation and trading circles), or even a Chinese or a pilot from India. Navigation between the Zanj of East Africa and the Indies had been established for centuries, and it is entirely possible that some stray mariner from Zanj could have turned up in Iberia. Whoever he was, it is certain, however, that this navigator's knowledge of land to the west had been gained, one way or another, from black Africans from the region of Cape Verde.

Not only was Columbus sure that land lay to the west of Cape Verde, but he said that he expected to find it at a distance of "750 leagues," or about 3,000 miles. This estimate cannot have been based upon cosmographic or astronomical considerations, for geographers of both Spanish and Portuguese examining commissions, relying upon the same cosmographical and astronomical sources as Columbus, consistently rejected his proposal because they knew well enough that the circumference of the earth placed the east coast of Cathay much further than 750 leagues from the west coast of Iberia. As Pohl remarks of Columbus' various presentations to geographers of Spain and Portugal:

The argument thus built up as to the short distance westwards to India, with its error of over six thousand English miles, was the critical one in his attempt to persuade the king of Portugal to sanction and finance his proposed expedition, for there were many who thought they knew, and really did know, near enough to the actual circumference of the earth to declare his project impossible.[13]

Columbus' project was impossible simply because the minimum of 9,000 miles separating "the Indies" from Portugal, as dictated by cosmological and astronomical sources, was beyond the range of sailing vessels of the day. A caravel could not make sufficient speed, nor carry enough food and water, to deliver a crew alive on a landfall 9,000 miles distant. The maximum ocean crossing possible was about 3,500 to 4,000 miles, assuming extremely favorable conditions.[14] No cosmographical or astronomical information indicated land at that distance westward from Iberia.

Yet Columbus apparently possessed sure knowledge of such a fact. In his various presentations to examining commissions in Spain and Portugal, Columbus maintained that if he did not find the Indies themselves "750 leagues" to the westwards he "might" find "some very beneficial island or continent" where ships could be reprovisioned to continue the voyage.

Columbus knew of land 750 leagues to the west of Cape Verde—750 leagues traveled by wind and current, not 750 leagues of geographical distance. It is interesting, therefore, that wind and currents would cast a Cape Verde mariner ashore on the coast of South America after a voyage of from 2,700 to 3,000 miles—or almost exactly Columbus' "750 leagues"—whereas the straight line distance separating Cape Verde from the New World is only slightly more than half that. Now, this knowledge could only have come from real maritime experience such as would be gained from expeditions into the west like those undertaken by sailors of Emperor Kankan Musa of Mali and his predecessor.

Yet Columbus dared not admit to possessing this certain knowledge whether he'd acquired it from hints in Perestrello's legacy, sailors' yarns, remarks of Senegal slaves in Portugal or a bookseller's chance knowledge of certain rare North African books—or, most probably, from a combination of all of these sources.

For if Columbus had convinced the experts of the Iberian examining commissions, monarchs would have seen little risk in it for Columbus and would simply have embarked on exploration without yielding to him the concessions he demanded. Columbus had to present his venture as one involving both plausibility and uncertainty. Without an element of gamble, there was no opportunity for him to make his fortune.

Columbus' major risk was that the known impossibility of his proposition, based on the "experts'" knowledge, made sponsorship of his expedition unlikely. He might never have been sponsored at all had it not been for a combination of his own determination and the success of Portuguese navigation around Africa. This success threatened Spain, and forced Spanish monarchs and business interests to take Columbus at his word. His venture, however implausible, represented Spain's only hope of duplicating Portuguese success.

Columbus was an able navigator and, if self-taught, knew as much and more about geography as any Iberian expert of the time. It is evident that he knew as well as the examining experts that "the Indies" lay more than 750 leagues to the west. But he knew that some land lay that distance to the west of Cape Verde, and since Iberian minds of the time were obsessed with the spice riches of "the Indies," Columbus simply equated the two in his various presentations.

It has been fashionable to believe that Columbus was ignorant of the fact that the land 3,000 miles to the west was a New World, and he *may* indeed have been so. Perhaps we should not place too much confidence in Pohl's assertion that "Columbus cannot be credited with the discovery of America *as a geographical fact* because he did not know of it and never conceived of it. To his dying day he insisted that he had reached Asia."[15]

Similar judgment has been written by Elizabeth Miller: "When he left Palos he was the foremost thinker of his day; when he landed on Watlings Island he was a bewildered, ignorant man on the threshold of immense facts,"[16] and, Pohl adds, "a threshold that he never passed."

Perhaps. However, in the agreement signed by Columbus and the Spanish crown on April 30, 1492, Columbus was entitled to take possession of and to govern in his lifetime any "islands and mainlands" he might discover before reaching Asia.

The same maritime tradition that gave Columbus certainty of land west of Cape Verde may also have given him rumors that high cultures flourished there. That this land could hardly be "the Indies" mattered little to him. Where there were civilized people there were riches and trade; and his agreement with the Spanish monarchs gave him trading rights in addition to governorship. His insistence that he had reached the Indies, when he had only discovered some tropical islands without high civilization, was expedient and good business. He may have known perfectly well that he was nowhere near the Indies, but he also knew that locating the developed people of this new land would take time, and further voyages. Columbus had to assure continued Spanish commitment until the riches and trade of this new land could be acquired. Furthermore, as early as 1489, da Gama's flagship *Sao Gabriel* had sailed the Indian Ocean and directly connected the Indies with Portugal, so Spain was desperate to cling to any possibility that might result in her gaining a foothold in the Indies.

We know now that Columbus did not "discover America," that the Vikings certainly preceded him and that, just possibly, Irish, Celtiberians and Phoenicians came before the Norse. Yet we are still confronted with the awesome fact that it was Columbus' voyages, and not earlier ones, that changed the course of history. Clearly, Columbus had discovered something. "Columbus discovered the ocean. His was a gift to Spain and to all of Europe of a practical sailing route across the Atlantic in which ships would find prevailing fair or following winds in each direction."[17]

Columbus was himself aware of his true achievement, knowing as he did that others had discovered the land 750 leagues westward of Cape Verde. Speaking of himself in the second person as the recipient of a divine vision, Columbus wrote: "Of the barriers of the Ocean sea, which were closed with such mighty chains, He gave thee the keys."[18] This statement by Columbus is still something of a distortion, but it is a fairer assessment than our ethnocentric insistence over so many years that Columbus discovered America. Columbus can truly lay claim to the discovery of the key to half the secret of Atlantic navigation.

True history insists that both knowledge of land to the west and knowledge of the equatorial currents and trade winds which would carry a ship to those shores was first gained by black African sailors setting out to the west from the region of Cape Verde.

Unidentified Emperor of Mali *painted on an early Portuguese map of West Africa. The emperor holds a nugget of gold, symbolic of the wealth the Portuguese believed to be in Mali.*

Only 150 years before Columbus' voyage, Ibn Amir Hajib asked Emperor Kankan Musa of Mali about navigation on the Atlantic and received this reply:

> The monarch who preceded me would not believe that it was impossible to discover the limits of the neighboring sea. He wished to know. He persisted in his plan. He caused the equipping of two hundred ships and filled them with men, and of another such number that were filled with gold, water and food for two years. He said to the commanders: Do not return until you have reached the end of the ocean, or when you have exhausted your food and water.
> They went away and their absence was long: none came back, and their absence continued. Then a single ship returned. We asked the captain of their adventures and their news. He replied: Sultan, we sailed for a long while until we met with what seemed to be a river with a strong current flowing in the open sea. My ship was last. The others sailed on, but as each of them came to that place they did not come back nor did they reappear; and I do not know what became of them. As for me, I turned where I was and did not enter the current.[19]

This description of what can only be the trade-wind-driven equatorial current is preserved in Omari's *Masalik-al-absad*. Columbus the bookseller may have stumbled on to this account, but a story of the same substance could have come to Portuguese mariners from slaves taken anywhere in the neighborhood of Cape Verde. In either case, Columbus would know that winds and currents existed which would push ships westward. While in Iceland, he would surely have noticed the prevailing westerly winds and the warm westerly current of the Gulf Stream. He could then reasonably conclude that the Atlantic could be crossed in each direction. That was the key to the barrier of the ocean sea.

There is no doubt that black Africans crossed the Atlantic to lands in the west, for how otherwise are we to explain the statues with Negroid features found at La Venta, or the representations of black men in the murals of the Temple of Warriors at Chichen Itza, or the presence of the tropical African bottle gourd in the New World? How otherwise can we explain that in both Central America and in the eastern foothills of the

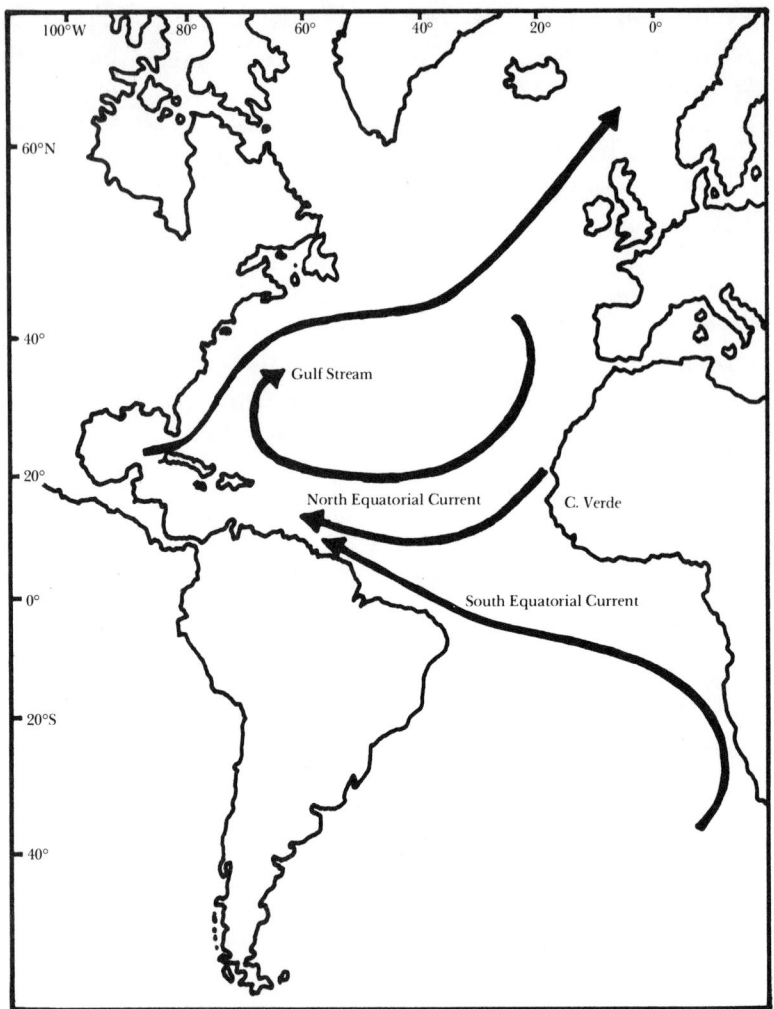

Wind and Currents of the Atlantic Ocean

Andes linguists find Negroid languages related to Mandinga, the language spoken by the people around Cape Verde?

There is also no doubt that, in spite of the contrary set of prevailing winds and currents, some few black African mariners returned from the New World to Cape Verde. Otherwise, how could Kankan Musa's predecessor be convinced that there were limits to the "neighboring sea"? How otherwise can we explain Columbus' conclusion that land lay 750 leagues westward of Cape Verde—a conclusion that was not only correct, but arrived at only after the Portuguese had reached the latitude and the people of Cape Verde? The evidence compels us to accept the idea that the success of Columbus' voyage owed much to the experience and knowledge gained by black mariners of Mali.

But if we accept that, then we must also be prepared to concede that this black discovery of America was the first such discovery by people of the Old World from the east. For the statues of La Venta with Negroid features date from the very beginning of Olmec culture, the foundation of Central American civilization. The black discovery of America must have occurred at least 3,000 years ago, at the very time when the earliest foundations of American civilization were begun. The cultural contact by black Africans is significant because it may have inspired the fledgling development of higher culture in America.

It is certain that later "white gods" in the guise of Egypto-Phoenicians, Carthaginians, Celtiberians and possibly Irish and Norse also influenced American cultures; they are remembered in legends from Mexico to Peru. It is said that the numbers of these white gods were small, yet they "brought civilization" to the peoples of America. A handful of Mediterranean or Celti-Norse visitors could not have founded empires with populations of millions from Mexico to Chile. The white gods came, and they brought civilized techniques, but it is equally certain that only great numbers of already highly cultured people could have adopted such techniques. There was culture in the Americas before the white gods arrived. Evidence suggests that black Africans had been present when this culture was first tentatively budding. Others—mostly the Amerindians themselves—contributed to the full flowering of a uniquely Amerindian culture.

But if the black discovery of America was significant in the cultural development in the New World, it also held significance for the cultural development of the Old World. For the black discovery of "land to the west" around 1000 B.C. was never entirely lost, though it passed through the traditions of many people. Columbus and the Portuguese in the years 1450 to 1492 A.D. had the same knowledge as the Carthaginians and Egyptians of about 500 to 600 B.C. and possibly earlier. As men of the Mediterranean crept out through the Pillars of Hercules and on down the African coast, they too would have come into contact with the mariners of Cape Verde and have concluded that there was land to the west. Egyptians and Phoenicians could have learned this about 600 B.C., when ships of Necho II circumnavigated Africa. Hanno the Carthaginian passed Cape Verde in 530 B.C. on his way to Mount Cameroon.

This knowledge was passed from the Phoenicians and their colonists to their Celtiberian neighbors in Iberia. And, when some of these Celtiberians migrated to Ireland and became Celts, they took this knowledge with them. The land to the west came to be called Iargalon—"the land beyond the sunset"—and in myth and legend it came to be known as a blessed land. Even when the migrations of peoples ended the ancient world and plunged Europe into the Dark Ages, knowledge of Iargalon was kept alive in Irish monasteries. Escaping from the pain and sin of a collapsed world, St. Brendan and other Irish *papar* set sail in their boats of leather for the blessed land they knew lay to the west. The recent voyage of Tim Severin and his crew in the *Brendan* shows that some of these seafaring priests could, indeed, have landed in the New World.[20]

When the Northmen sacked Irish monasteries in the seventh century, knowledge of western lands passed to the Vikings, and they set sail to discover Greenland and Markland and Vinland the Good.

Which brings us full circle to Columbus, in Iceland in 1477, where the tradition of land to the west passed on to change history. Yet the origin of the tradition seems clear enough, and Columbus himself heard reports from Cape Verde, the source of the tradition that had endured for thousands of years among many peoples.

If black Africans did, in fact, discover America, how is it that not one inkling of this achievement survives in the common knowledge of average, educated Western people?

Part of the answer is that Columbus and others after him had good reason to keep certain secrets for years after the first voyage. Both Columbus and Spain sought more than trade and riches. Spain wanted to take possession of new lands, and Columbus wanted to govern them. To admit that such lands had been previously discovered by mariners of another recognized monarch, even a remote African one, would have jeopardized Spain's claims in the New World. No hint of any previous discovery could be allowed until the Spanish presence in the newly discovered territory was strong enough to withstand challenge by force.

Furthermore, other nations, Portugal in particular, sought a "legal" pretext for encroaching on the Spanish triumph. If Spain had not, in fact, "discovered" the New World, other nations would be within their rights to take whatever land they could, as Spain's claim to it would be spurious.

But there was another political consideration. In 1492, the Spanish finally defeated the Moors. War with the Moors had raged for centuries, mortgaging Spain's monetary resources and energy, and preventing her from entering the Age of Exploration as early as Portugal or with the same dedication. The Empire of Mali might be far removed from Spain, but the Moors across the Straits of Gibraltar were not. Nor was Mali far from the minds of North African Arabs. Islam had long been entrenched in the Empire of Mali and there were close relations, both friendly and unfriendly, between the Moors of North Africa and the Western Sudanese. It is at least conceivable that the Moors themselves could have challenged part of Spain's claim to her transatlantic possessions, fomented strife among the Moors remaining in Spain, and hindered shipping in the vicinity of Gibraltar. So it was wise for both Spain and Columbus to bury all reference to possible prior discovery of the New World by sailors of an Islamic empire.

These political considerations helped to guarantee that any black discovery of land across the Atlantic would be quickly and conveniently forgotten. But no such discovery could have been forgotten so completely without the help of the slave trade, which would ultimately form the basis of the European view of all black African achievements.

Beginning in 1444, Portuguese slave depredations along the coast of Africa grew quickly to unbelievable proportions. It has been estimated that "one million three hundred and eighty-nine thousand slaves were taken from the coast of Angola alone in the years between 1486 and 1641."[21] And the Portuguese were not the only predators. "Liverpool records of a century later show that in the eleven years of 1783 to 1793, about nine hundred Liverpool voyages were made for slaving and carried over three hundred thousand slaves."[22]

Not only was the coast of West Africa literally denuded of population—for those who were not taken by the slavers fled inland—but the cohesion of inland societies was destroyed. Empires collapsed under the social pressure and the customs of people degenerated.

Ibn Battuta described the Mali Negroes about 1300 A.D., before slavery began:

[They] are seldom unjust, and have a greater abhorrence of injustice than any other people. Their sultan shows no mercy to anyone who is found guilty of the least act of it. There is complete security in the country. Neither traveler nor inhabitant in it has anything to fear from robbers or men of violence. They do not confiscate the property of any white man who dies in their country, even if it be uncounted wealth. On the contrary, they give it into the charge of some trustworthy person among the whites, until the rightful heir takes possession of it.[23]

After four centuries of the slave trade, Commander Bacon described Benin in 1897:

Truly has Benin been called a city of blood. Its history is one long record of savagery of the most debased kind. . . . Blood was everywhere. . . . On the right was a crucifixion tree with a double crucifiction on it, the two poor wretches stretched out facing west, with their arms bound together in the middle. . . . At the base were skulls and bones, literally strewn about, the debris of former sacrifices, and down every main road were two or more human sacrifices.[24]

The insatiable appetite for slaves was not all that Europeans brought to Africa. They also brought a savagery in warfare that other peoples, including Africans, have been able to equal.

Speaking of the coming of Vasco da Gama and the Portuguese to East Africa, Basil Davidson writes:

They cut savagely across those many complex strands of commerce which centuries had woven between these myriad ports and peoples of the east; and they wrecked the whole fabric of that trade, leaving behind them, when their force was spent, little but ruin and disruption.

Schooled in the bitter rivalries of Europe, they fell upon these tolerant and easy-going civilizations of the Indian Ocean with a ferocity and violence that were like nothing seen here through many centuries.[25]

The effect on the Zanj of East Africa was the same as the effect on the cultures, like that of Mali, on the west coast. Faced with this awesome brutality, the population fled, and cities were abandoned to the jungle. People once as civilized as the Portuguese themselves became debased.

So it was that, as the first explorers pushed inland from the deserted coasts in the 1800s they found savage, tribal people, and it was too easy to believe that they had always been that way, that "for countless centuries, while all the pageant of history swept by, the African remained unmoved—in primitive savagery."[26] David Hume wrote: "No ingenious manufactures among them, no arts, no sciences. No approach to the civilization of his white fellow creatures whom he imitates as a monkey does a man."

As late as 1958, Sir Arthur Kirby, commissioner for British East Africa in London, could blithely say: "In the last sixty years—little more than the lifetime of some people in this room—East Africa has developed from a completely primitive country, in many ways more backward than the Stone Age."

What the Europeans perpetrated in Africa, they repeated in the New World.

> In what used to be called Hispaniola (today Haiti and Santo Domingo) the native population numbered about one hundred thousand in 1492, but had dropped to 200 about a century later, since people died of horror and disgust at European civilization even more than of smallpox and physical ill-treatment.[27]

And, after the destruction, murder and enslavement, later generations of Europeans and colonials would look upon the few wretched survivors as "lazy, filthy pagans, of bestial morals, no better than dogs, and fit only for slavery, in which state alone there might be some hope of converting them to Christianity."[28]

With such attitudes, it seemed natural that even the "knowledge establishment" of western science created myths of Amerindian and African inadequacy in almost every area of culture. It is only within the last few decades that some of these myths have been shattered, but they still dominate our textbooks and form the preconceptions of the average Western person. It is perhaps not too unjust to predict that future generations may well delve into some of our most respected textbooks, tally the errors and misconceptions, and conclude that Westerners educated between 1860 and 1960 represent the most ignorant of all generations on matters of basic human history.

Characteristically, it has been those outside the knowledge establishment who have striven, and sometimes succeeded, in correcting our myths. Thor Heyerdahl did so when he demonstrated the voyaging capabilities of the Amerindian Incas of Peru by crossing to Polynesia aboard an Inca balsa raft. Yet, only in a later experiment, in 1953, did Heyerdahl build a second balsa raft, and off the coast of Ecuador prove that the ancient Inca method of *guara* navigation permitted the raft to be sailed to windward as well as downwind. Although this experiment is still largely unknown to the general public and to many specialists, we are confronted with the irony that the Incas possessed vessels superior to those of the contemporary Spanish in every major respect: seaworthiness, carrying capacity, and the ability to sail to windward.

With the success of the *Ra II* expedition, Heyerdahl demonstrated the sea-going ability of the reed boat and proved that men using vessels of papyrus—early Egyptians, Phoenicians or people of Lixus on the coast of Morocco—could, indeed, have crossed from North Africa to the New World.

What Heyerdahl demonstrated on behalf of the Incas remains to be proved for the black Africans: namely that they possessed both the capability of crossing oceans and a sufficiently high cultural level to have contributed to the initial and early development of civilization in the Americas.

A cynical modern reader might well ask: "If the Incas and the black Africans had such voyaging capability, why is it that our ships came to them and not theirs to us?" The answer seems to lie not in capability but in temperament and inclination. Whereas all peoples have demonstrated aggression and frustration and the lust for expansion, Western white men seem to possess the greatest degree of aggression; our geographical expansion and the magnitude of our cruelties are evidence of this. We have voyaged—and murdered, enslaved and tortured—on a greater scale than any other people.[29]

In tracing the cultural developments in both black Africa and in the Americas to show the contact between them, I will draw upon archeological evidence as well as upon tradition in trying to redress an unjust history. But I will be wary of primitive myths and savage distortions, for much primitive myth is enshrined in our own science and much savagery emanates from our own psychology.

2

The Niger
and the Nile

Our knowledge of the history of Africa south of the Sahara is a void. Almost nothing is known of Negro culture before about 500 A.D. Arab accounts of West Africa and East Africa of about 700 A.D. suggest that things were much different then than they were in the 1800's when Europeans pushed into the interior and found, after four centuries of slave trade, confused and disorganized societies of savages.

Even the Negroes themselves are a mystery. Although Africa seems to have been the earliest cradle of humanity, the black race appears to be the latest distinctive expression of it. American anthropologist Carleton Coon wrote in 1962: "The origin of the African Negroes, and of the Pygmies, is the greatest unsolved mystery in the field of racial study. . . . Negroes and Pygmies appeared as if out of nowhere."[1]

The black Africans materialized about 5000 B.C.

Some time around 5000 B.C. new types of humanity appeared in Africa. The Negro or Negroid type was prominent among these. His earliest remains have come, so far, from much the same African latitudes: a fossilized skull and some other fragments from a Middle Stone Age site near Khartoum in the Sudan, and another skull and some bones from beneath thick clay at Asselar, some two hundred miles northeast of Timbuktu in the western Sudan.[2]

Which is to say that the "black" Africans seem to have originated not in the tropics but in the area that is now the dry desert of the southern Sahara stretching almost from the Atlantic to Ethiopia. The Sahara, now desert, may hold the key to many mysteries. Aerial photographs tell us that wide rivers and lakes once sparkled where now only mirages shimmer. The Sahara may have been the birthplace of both Negroes and early

Egyptian culture in the days, thousands of years ago, when it was fertile. It may be that as the Sahara began to dry up, a process that seems to have begun in the north and spread to the south, the people who lived in this once-parkland area migrated away in all directions.

Some went directly south into the tropical fringe of West Africa around the shores of the Atlantic. They established themselves in the forested region of tropical West Africa as early as 3000 B.C., and they brought a relatively high Saharian cultural level with them.[3] Others retreated to the northeast, and settled along the upper Nile, in Nubia. They eventually migrated farther. Some traveled west in the sub-Saharan fringe to join those who arrived in West Africa earlier.

Others went north, into what became Egypt. "An analysis of some eight hundred skulls from pre-dynastic Egypt—that is, from the lower valley of the Nile before about 3000 B.C.—shows that at least a third of them were Negroes or ancestors of the Negroes whom we know."[4]

Therefore, much of what we consider Egyptian culture, technology and religion may actually have developed in the Sahara and been transported into tropical West Africa and to Nubia before it reached the Nile delta.

We know nothing of the cultures of the Sahara of about 5000 B.C. We have only tantalizing hints. In 1958, French explorer Henri Lhote revealed an astonishing collection of rock paintings and engravings that he had recovered from the mountains of Tassili in what is now the absolute middle of the Sahara, a point almost equidistant from the Nile delta, Nubia and Cape Verde. The art included vital and realistic representations of tropical and savannah animals now long vanished, sensitive portraiture of men and women of both black and white races, pictures of two-wheeled chariots with horses shown in the flying gallop of later Cretan style, and boats of what we would later call "Egyptian" papyriform shape. Lhote's work at Tassili showed that no less than sixteen different cultures flourished near that site, either successively or concurrently.[5]

The age of this Sahara culture? No one knows for sure. A mystifying mixture of epochs seems to exist at this place, and there does not seem to be a way of dating these drawings with any degree of accuracy.

But perhaps the legends of people are, after all, the surest guide:

There is practically no well-known people in West Africa without its legend of an eastern or northern origin in the remote past.[6]

"God's Land" with all its great ancestral spirits lay, for dynastic Egypt, neither in the east nor in the north, but far to the south and west.[7]

If West Africans hold that their origins were in the northeast, and Egyptians remember theirs as being in the southwest, it seems reasonable to suppose that the epicenter of cultural beginnings was somewhere in the Sahara, perhaps not far from the mountains of Tassili.

Perhaps it is not too much of a digression to mention that some of the Saharan refugees may have fled north across the Mediterranean. We should not forget that Greeks claimed that they had learned how to hitch four horses to a chariot from the Libyans. This brings to mind the chariots painted on rocks at Tassili. Also, the Greek goddess Athena originally came out of Africa from Libya.[8]

If some of these northward-fleeing refugees turned eastward across the Mediterranean, reaching Greece and influencing conceptions of religion there, some also tended west across the Mediterranean and reached Ireland through Iberia, bringing religious beliefs and a number of similar gods, goddesses and heroes and heroines to Celtic tradition. Robert Graves considers that the Tuatha de Danaan, one of the first Celtic peoples of Ireland, came from Libya originally and reached Ireland about 2500 to 2000 B.C. The *Book of Ballymote* does in fact list an alphabet described as African, but this was judged to be medieval monkish gibberish by modern scholars until Libyan dialects were deciphered in the 1960's. Then it transpired that, sure enough, the African script preserved in the *Book of Ballymote* was indeed ancient Libyan.[9]

It has been said that Africa gave the gods to Egypt and that Greece received them second-hand from Egypt. This is the truth, but it is a truth with complications. It appears that the earliest religious conceptions of Celt, Cretan, Mycenaean Greek and Egyptian alike came out of the Sahara via Libyan refugees at about the same time. Subtle refinements and similarities then passed between the nations of the Mediterranean at a later date.

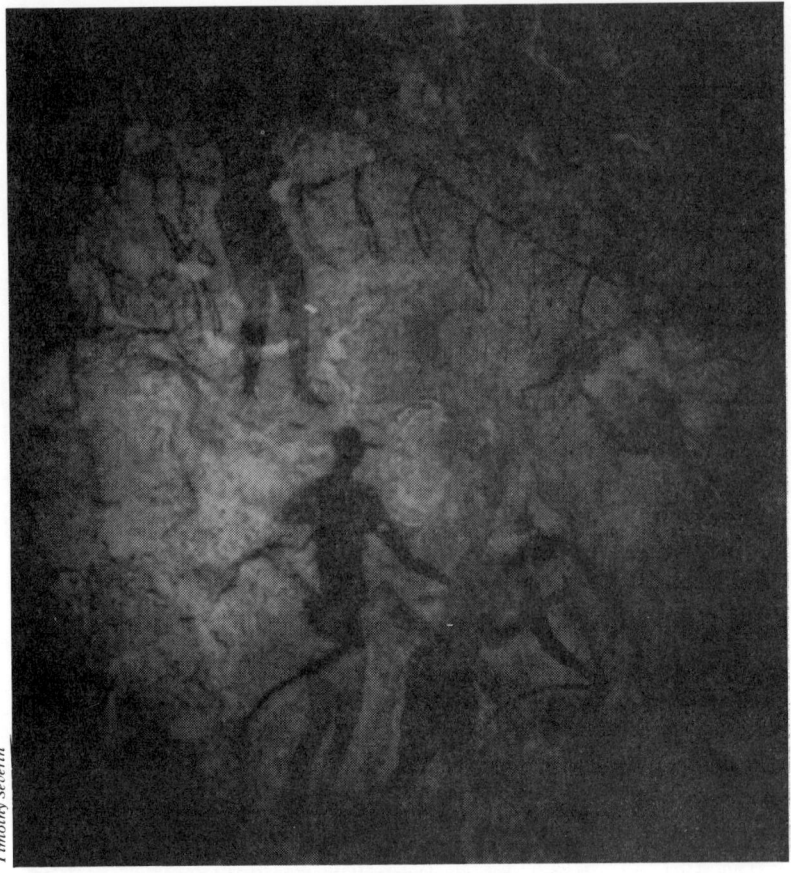

Ancient fishermen in the Sahara. *Rock drawings show a man hauling in a net. The Sahara was once well watered and fertile; and it is possible that ancient civilization began here. Peoples migrated as the Sahara turned to sand, taking the seed of civilization with them in all directions. The black Africans seem to have evolved in the Sahara about the time these rock paintings were created, and certainly contributed to this primal Saharan culture complex.*

The same Saharan refugees who reached Europe and the Mediterranean also went south to tropical West Africa bringing the same gods. It is not surprising then that amazing parallels of religious belief, of heroic legend and of custom exist between people as widely separated as the Irish, black Africans, Egyptians and Greeks.

Take, for example, the serpent—specifically the python—which black West Africans considered to represent wisdom. This python became a cobra among peoples who lived in drier areas where there were no pythons. We find cobras of wisdom protruding from the foreheads of Pharaonic statuary and among Ethiopian sculptures. One of the temples of Naga in Nubia is adorned with a magnificent large coiled serpent, probably a python, and it immediately recalls the "feathered serpent" architectural motif occurring in Meso-America.

As with the serpent, so with the ram. Alexander of Macedon, who aspired to the godhead, adopted the ram's horns of Zeus Ammon, but postponed his official deification until it could be accomplished by the priests of a Libyan shrine. Alexander went to the Libyan shrine because of oracular advice given by a female seer or "pythoness" at Dodona in Greece. Amen-Ra was the ram-headed sun god of the Egyptians and Osiris was also ram headed. But the ram was also the symbol of Zeus' thunder and lightning in black Africa:

> The Mandinka of Western Sudan consider that the god of storm and thunder takes earthly shape as a ram. The Yoruba national god, Shango, appears with a ram's mask and is equally god of storm and thunder. . . . Divine rams, in one guise or another, carry on right down through the Cameroons into the remote basin of the Congo. . . . Priestly breastplates, from Yorubaland in southern Nigeria of the medieval period, recall similar models dedicated to Amun in dynastic Egypt.[10]

We see vestiges of the concepts of ram and serpent preserved in various guises throughout the Ancient World, although the cohesion of the symbolism, which originated in the Sahara, is probably forever lost to us. But this age-old Saharan symbolism survived even to affect our own religious tradition. The Arabs refer to Moses as Dhul Karnain, or "two-horned," and Moses probably wore a ram-headed mask. Moses also carried the "Ne-Esthan" (in the Greek Septuagint spelling), a device in the likeness of the Brazen Serpent. As leader of a diverse people, Moses may have tried to combine the symbols of two powerful cults for political reasons, but he succeeded in transcending both when he attributed to his single God, Jehovah, the attributes of both the power of "thunder and lightning and storm" symbolized by the ram and the wisdom symbolized by the serpent. Just as Alexander became two-horned when he assumed divinity at the Libyan shrine, so Moses became an "alexander"

Basil Davidson

when, with his ram's horns and serpent device, he led the Israelites in the desert. For alexander means a "warder off of evil from men." It is not by accident that both Alexander and Moses are known to Arabs as Dhul Karnain, nor that, at the other end of the European world, in Wales, the two heroes are frequently connected in poetic allusion, such as in the *Hanes Taliesin*.[11]

We see in these far-flung scraps of legends a barely discernible common theme weary with age, wisps of memory torn by time and migrations of people. But it seems that at one time, in Saharan dawns of the fifth millennium before the Great Pan— himself a ram—died, the fragments that we see now once

The Sun as Ram—Amen Ra. *Baluba sculpture from the Congo (left) and Hellenistic coin showing Alexander of Macedon after assuming divinity. The cult of sun-as-ram was widespread in the Middle East and Africa. West African breastplates resemble those of Egyptian priests of Amen Ra.*

reflected the accepted reality of the world with man and nature joined. That world view was mirrored in Saharan waters long since evaporated. The mists rose, and scattered to become memories from which nations counted their beginnings.

Evidence suggests that black Africans, driven south of the Sahara, participated in molding this world view as it was seen and lived in the morning of remembered time. The fact that these black Africans were subsequently separated from "us" by the Sahara does not mean that they were separated from us conceptually as we used to be and perhaps as we should have remained.

In the ancient world of Eurasia and Egypt, and no less among black Africans south of the Niger and Senegal rivers, we perceive a common ancient theme: a generalized worship of the sun and the earth as the two basic elements of life on this planet—as indeed they are. A sun-god was represented by an earthly divine king; but the female principle was revered by making the succession to kingship matrilinear, and by representations of fertility and love goddesses. Beneath this sexually balanced basic belief, certain symbols were accepted as illustrating more specific powers: we have rams of thunder, lightning and storm; we have serpents of convenient species representing wisdom; we have a host of other gods, goddesses and semi-divine beings who personify various aspects of love, hate, greed, benevolence, fate, war, etc., and who are depicted in a variety of guises.

And if we see certain of these concepts and specific representations duplicated in the New World, we do not have to immediately assume contact by men of the Mediterranean, because, having come originally from the same cultural crucible in the Sahara, black Africans could have supplied most of the basic parallels equally well. Worship of the sun and of a divine sun-king is not only Egyptian, but also West African.[12]

> The pre-Columbian Toadstool-god Tlaloc (of Mexico), represented as a toad with a serpent head-dress, has for thousands of years presided at the communal eating of the hallucinogenic toadstool *psilocybe*.... Tlaloc's European counterpart, Dionysus, shares too many of his mythical attributes for coincidence: they must be versions of the same deity; though at what period cultural contact took place between the Old World and the New is debatable.[13]

West African gods with the same attributes, portrayed in the same way, could have supplied the template for Tlaloc just as well as Dionysus could.

But, back to West African history. The Nok figurine culture of central Nigeria shows indisputably that by 3000 B.C. people somehow related to the Sahara culture of Tassili were established in West Africa. By 1200 B.C. bronze had come south of the Sahara and was being worked along with gold; by this time too, the lost-wax method of casting was known and used. Cotton was being woven.

And that is all that can be said. The archeology of tropical

Africa is in its infancy. The first Nok figurine was found only in 1931, the next three in 1944, and an understanding of the culture that produced this naturalistic art is still far from complete.

> Europeans had often thought, for example, that Negro peoples produced no native tradition of anthropomorphic art—of the more or less natural portrayal of humanity....
> What peoples made such fine heads in terra cotta more than two thousand years ago is anybody's guess; although some of the portrait heads suggest that the Nok people were the direct ancestors of some of the peoples who live in central Nigeria today.[14]

Doubtless, many cultures comparable to Nok existed all over West Africa, and it is probably only the lack of intensive excavation that has created our historical void. It is a simple fact that between the Nok culture and the beginning of medieval Arab and European accounts of West Africa we presently know nothing. But there is room for speculation grounded in known facts. First, from the earliest times of the Nok figurine culture, there would have been at least some contact with Egypt to the east. About 1200 B.C., there arose to the south of Egypt, in the present day Sudan, the kingdom of Kush. (Actually, it seems to have been more of a queendom.) The first capital of Kush seems to have been Musawarat, but the capital was later moved to Meroë. Excavation has barely begun in Meroë. Even after the first large-scale archeological research in 1958-59, undertaken by the Sudanese government, it is estimated that only one-tenth of the area of Meroë has been surveyed, much less excavated. Aside from Musawarat and Meroë, other Kushite cities included Naga, Napata and Nuri.

Kush was a black African state, although it seems to have borrowed very much from Egypt in the north, at least in terms of its monumental building and sculpture. But it is best to be careful here. It may be that the seeds of civilization reached Egypt from Kush and not the other way about, although the seed certainly flourished more luxuriantly and more rapidly once it reached the Nile delta. The Kushites seem to have been sun-worshipers like the Egyptians and boasted a huge Temple of the Sun of which Herodotus had heard rumors 2,400 years ago. There probably was a divine kingship, at least in the beginning, but the line was matrilinear. By about 500 B.C. the balance of sexual power apparently shifted and Kush came to be ruled mostly by queens. The Kushite city of Napata was a center for the worship of Amun-Ra or the "sun as ram."

This is about all that is known of Kush in the Bronze Age. But there's no doubt that Kush would have influenced the culture of West Africa more than Egypt directly, if only because Kushite cities were at least 1,000 miles closer by travel around the southern rim of the Sahara. By about 700 B.C. the kingdom of Kush became powerful enough to conquer Egypt itself, establishing the 25th or Ethiopian Dynasty. The first pharaohs of this dynasty ruled from the Mediterranean "to the borders of modern Ethiopia and, for all we know, Uganda too" . . . and this statement reflects our uncertainty about everything except the northern Kush-Egyptian border. Its western frontiers may well have reached as far as Lake Chad. Its influence certainly did.

It is thought that iron was first smelted about 1500 B.C. somewhere in Anatolia or in the foothills of the Caucasus. The first of the ancients to put iron to good use were the Assyrians, and with it they overwhelmed much of the Near East because their opponents were armed with bronze. Egypt was conquered by Assyria about 650 B.C. Ashurbanipal ended the Ethiopian Dynasty and drove the Kushite armies south.

Gradually, however, other peoples adopted the use of iron, and the Kushites lagged behind no one. The first iron object found in Kush came from the burial of Harsiotef and dates to about 360 B.C. Barely 150 years later, Kush was a major producer of iron, especially in the city of Meroë. "Mountains of iron slag enclose the city mounds on their northern and eastern sides, and excavation has brought to light the furnaces in which the iron was smelted and fashioned into tools and weapons."[15] In fact, Meroë was a sort of Pittsburgh or Birmingham of the old Sudan, and its slag-heaps became just as characteristic of its culture as the pyramids of former rulers.

We do not know for certain when the use of iron reached tropical West Africa and the sub-Saharan savannahs. Experts guess at about 100 to 500 A.D. When the curtain goes up on West African history, as recorded in Arab sources dating from 700 A.D., iron-using centralized empires are already in existence, but no one knows how long such polities existed before they came to literate Arab notice. El Fazari first mentions the land of Ghana shortly after 800 A.D. and describes it as a "land of

Medieval West African Mounted Warrior

gold." About 250 years later, El Zouhi explained that most peoples of West Africa "know not iron and fight with bars of ebony" and that the Ghanians "can defeat them because they fight with swords and lances."[16] Ghana was the first large centralized empire we know of in West Africa that arose because of the revolution brought about by iron, but simultaneously other West Africans were discovering the metal and would put it to use.

Although we know much more about these Iron Age West African people than we do about empires that must have flourished previously, we really know every little: Ghana was a center of power as of 800 A.D.; a little later and to the west, the Empire of Mali began its rise until between 1200 and 1400 A.D. it was the undisputed power in this part of the world; then, far to the east in the region of Lake Chad, the empire of Kanem-Bornu existed from about 800 A.D. or earlier until the 1600s; while Sonni Ali made Sanghay the most powerful West African state between about 1450 and 1550, he and his successors ruling from the city of Gao on the Niger.

We know that in their heydays, these West African states were more powerful than many medieval European countries. "Tunka Manin is master of a great empire and of a power which is formidable." Their cities of Mali, according to Arab visitors, were "filled with fine houses and solid buildings," and they acquired immense wealth by trading gold from the south for the salt of the north. It is said that major cities of this region boasted medieval populations of up to 30,000 people—about the size of early medieval Paris—and that, at the apogee of its power, an emperor of Mali could command 200,000 mail-clad warriors armed with steel weapons.[17]

The power of various West African states was sufficiently formidable to stop the Islamic *jihad* at the southern boundary of the Sahara in spite of the fact that, in addition to religious fervor, the Almorovids had an additional incentive in the gold possessed by these black empires. Although invariably victorious from Spain to Central Asia, Arab armies of the Middle Ages were stopped in Africa. Their victories were rare and costly, and they never achieved a lasting conquest until 1591, when Moroccan armies of El Mansur defeated those of Askia Ishak of Songhay. But even this might not have occurred if European slaving along the coasts of Africa had not weakened these inland empires. Ravaged by the Europeans on the coasts and by powerful Arabic armies from the north, the African empires succumbed and the people reverted to tribalism.

During the 800 years of political independence from Islamic rulers to the north, many West Africans adopted the Islamic faith. Some emperors of Mali and Songhay were Moslems, but some were not and continued to practice their old religions. Yet, in adopting Islam, the Africans changed it in accord with their traditional beliefs. For example, the status of women

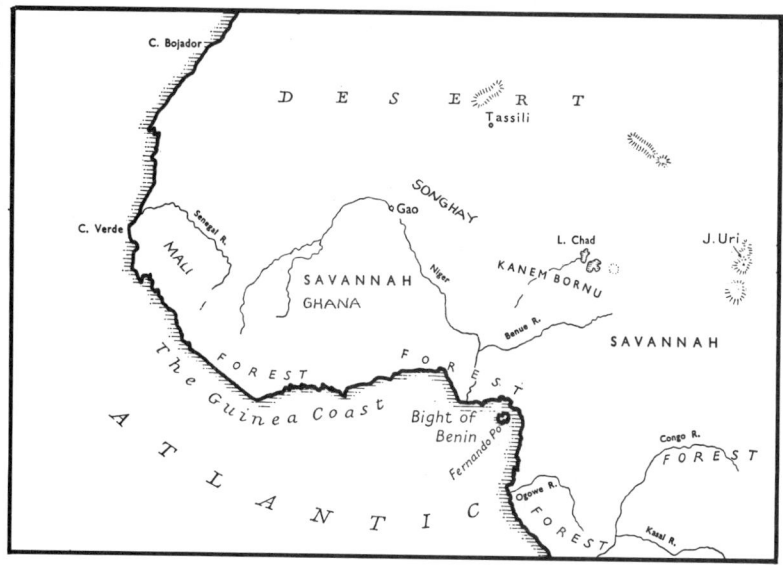

West Africa

among black African Moslems was much higher than in other Arabic lands—and much higher than that of women in Europe during the years between 800 and 1500 A.D. The ancient African tradition of matrilinear succession and respect for women maintained itself in black Africa even within Islam. Ibn Battuta, an Arab visitor to Mali, was a bit shocked at this. Writing about 1300 A.D., he says:

> Their men show no sign of jealousy whatsoever. No one claims descent from his father, but on the contrary from his mother's brother. A person's heirs are his sister's sons, not his own sons. This is a thing which I have seen nowhere in the world except among the Indians of Malabar. But *those* are heathens; *these* people are Muslims, punctilious in observing the hours of prayer, studying books of law, and in memorizing the Koran. Yet their women show no bashfulness before men and do not veil themselves, though they are assiduous in attending prayer.[18]

By the 1700s most traces of indigenous high culture in West Africa had been erased, and by late in the century we have Mungo Park's narrative of slavery and savage chaos all through the country of the Niger. After Park came the other well-known

African explorers of the 1800s who brought back to civilization our current view of the "dark continent."

In writing about Africa, as Basil Davidson has aptly put it, one has to "steer between the rock of prejudice and the whirlpool of romance." The course is difficult because there is precious little known that is useful for guidance. How civilized was Africa before European and Arab slaving destroyed much of its culture? Could the West Africa of 1000 B.C. or so have been sophisticated enough to influence the development of civilization in the Americas?

There is absolutely no hard evidence that such a degree of civilization existed in West Africa about 3,000 years ago. The evidence remains buried in the ground and awaits archeological discovery, but there is little doubt that it is there. The high medieval cultures of West Africa must have originated in long experience of large-scale political and economic organization. We may reasonably infer the existence of high cultures there because of known migration routes of peoples out of the drying Sahara.

We know of the civilization built by black Africans in Kush. In 947 A.D. El Mas'udi wrote in *Meadows of Gold and Mines of Gems*:

> ... the sons of Kush, the son of Canaan, traveled toward the west and crossed the Nile. There they separated. Some of them, the Nubians and the Beja and the Zanj, turned to the rightward, between the east and the west; but the others, very numerous, marched toward the setting sun.

This is a garbled legend. These sons of Kush—or their culture—had originated in the west, in the dried Sahara. The inhabitants also scattered after the fall of Kush at the hands of Axum (now modern Ethiopia) about 300 A.D. But most of the Kushites probably did travel westward because they had always trickled westward around the southern rim of the Sahara into West Africa and because they knew that westward lay their origins.

It is reasonable to infer that in tropical West Africa as elsewhere, civilization developed from seeds carried by Saharan migrants from the Tassili cultures that Lhote discovered. If we know that these seeds of culture came from the Sahara to Egypt, to Nubia, across the Mediterranean to Greece—and to the

"Celts" in North Africa who later carried the seeds of culture across the Mediterranean to the "Celtiberians" of Iberia and on to Ireland—why not to tropical West Africa? In fact, we know that this was so: the Nok figurine culture dating back to 3000 B.C. tells us that the seeds of civilization reached West Africa, too. Are we to suppose that everywhere but West Africa the seeds sprouted into civilization? If so, it is almost certain that we have hit the rock of prejudice and that our cargo of historical conception is in jeopardy.

It would also be bad navigation to suppose that an extremely high civilization, comparable to that of dynastic Egypt, flourished in West Africa during the thousands of silent years for which we have no written or archeological records. For, if the black Africans appeared only about 7,000 years ago, they cannot have been very numerous between 5,000 and 3,000 years ago when they were driven into the savannahs and forests south of the Sahara and began to establish themselves in a new and challenging environment. They cannot have been very numerous when the American archeological record shows that black men reached the New World. In fact, Africa has never been very thickly populated, and in their long migrations southward to people the continent, black Africans did not reach the Cape of Good Hope by land before the Europeans reached it in their ships.

Further, although there are great rivers in West Africa, none is as large as the Nile, and all take their sources from an increasingly drying hinterland south of the desert. When they overflow, West African rivers do not leave behind them rich silt as does the Nile, and opportunities for agriculture are limited. The soil is so shallow in most parts of West Africa that the people, after laboriously clearing the land, must still relocate every few years as the soil loses its productive capacity. The seeds of civilization were doubtless brought here but found a much less suitable ground for flowering than in other places.

We may be sure that bronze reached the black Africans very soon after it was in general use throughout the ancient world. Yet, though Africa is rich in metals, including copper, West Africa happens to be poor in metals that can be alloyed with copper to make bronze. What Herodotus records about "Ethiopia" is no less true of West Africa: "in Ethiopia the rarest and most precious metal is bronze" and prisoners "were bound in golden chains."[14]

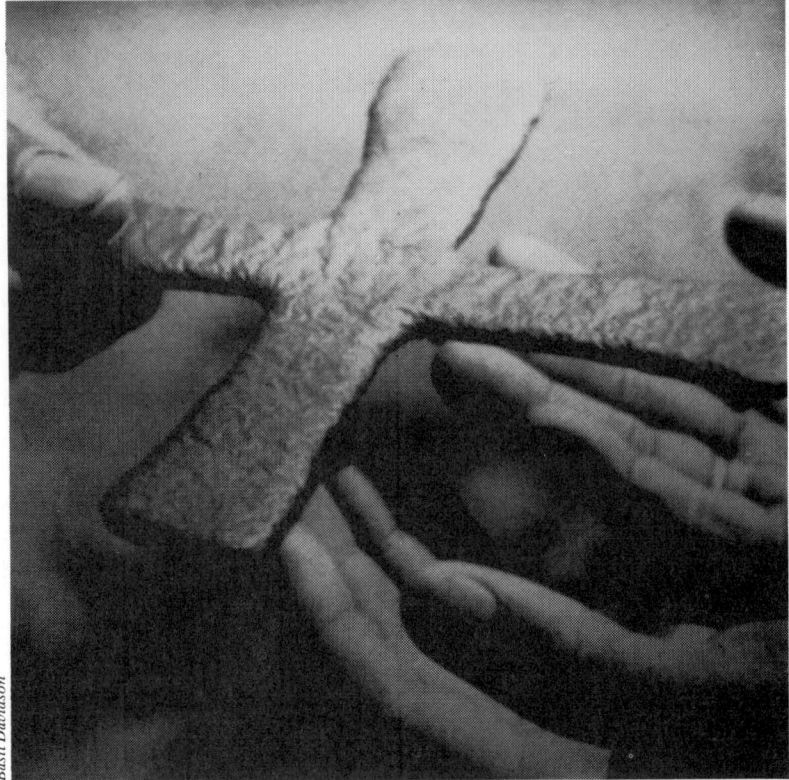

Pre-European copper ingot from central Africa. *The Africans could smelt and work copper and gold from a very early time, but had little of the metals needed to alloy to copper to make bronze. Because of this lack of bronze, the Africans used wood, stone and bone for tools; but used copper and gold for adornment. Later, the Africans adopted iron and exported great quantities of high quality iron to India through East African ports.*

It is said that one ruler of Mali possessed a golden nugget so huge that a horse could be tethered securely to it, and certainly the Arabs knew that West Africa was a land of gold. There is no doubt, therefore, that the black Africans could smelt and work metals from the earliest times, but they could produce bronze only rarely. The black Africans possessed the knowledge of working bronze, but scarcely had the opportunity to put it in practice. They worked copper and gold into the only things for which these metals are useful—jewelry and statuary—and their workmanship in metal was of a high quality, but they were forced to use wood, stone and bone for tools. There was no African Bronze Age comparable to the use of this metal in other ancient cultures. I have used the term Bronze Age elsewhere in my discussion because the rest of the world was in such an age when the black Africans first set sail for the New World.

This natural lack of bronze-making materials partly explains the astonishing avidity with which the Africans adopted the use of iron, a metal with which they and their continent were richly provided. Far to the south, in the East African coastal region, iron was produced in such quantity that it formed the largest item of a very brisk trade with India between 500 and 1500 A.D., a network of commerce upon which a true civilization was built with many towns of beauty—as the earliest Portuguese visitors attested. This civilization of the Indian Ocean shore was a product, again, of black African and Arab cooperation. The people of this culture were called the Zanj. Their iron was famous throughout the Indian-Arab world, for from it the finest quality Damascus steel was made.

If we seek to compare the black African cultural level to some people familiar to us, possibly the best comparison is offered by the ancient Britons or Celts before the coming of the Iron Age. We know that these people were not howling savages but possessed a great fund of astronomical and mathematical knowledge, a rich literature that was originally created and transmitted in a completely oral tradition, and a sophisticated and complicated religious system. They, too, worked bronze and knew weaving. They built, as did the black Africans, impressive structures that were partly religious and partly astronomical in nature. They built large palaces on occasion, but the majority of the people lived in relatively simple huts. Although metal and cloth were known, wood and stone were used for many tools and weapons, while skins were often used for clothing. Like the Africans, the Celts seem to have concentrated on religious and literary development rather than technological development.

Both peoples had distinctive languages but possessed no alphabet that we have discovered. They borrowed letters from other peoples in order to write. The black Africans adopted Arabic script and adapted it to their languages in Mali, Songhay and in the land of the Zanj. The Celts adopted the Roman alphabet.

Recalibrated carbon dating now shows that the megaliths of northwest Europe are older than the Egyptian pyramids, and it is very possible that the mathematical and astronomical knowledge needed to build monumentally came originally out of the lost Saharan world and traveled with the Celts more directly and more quickly than it did to Egypt.[20] There is every reason to believe that the intellectual foundation of civilization existed among the Celts and black Africans no less than among the earliest Egyptians and Sumerians. The difference in subsequent development was due to limitations of environment: we should not be fooled into assuming the Celts and black Africans were *culturally* retarded, though their material lifestyle may have been so.

The final conclusion must be that the black Africans of about 1000 B.C. possessed the knowledge required to inspire the earliest American cultures. Their knowledge of metal-working, for example, was advanced enough to have inspired the American metal traditions from earliest times. In fact, their knowledge could have been put to more immediate use in America than in Africa itself, since bronze-making alloys exist more plentifully in the eastern foothills of the Andes than in the Sahelia. It is interesting to note that although the American cultures produced excellent metal work, they, like the black Africans, used metal—even bronze—mostly for ornaments rather than for tools and weapons. The men of the Mediterranean did the reverse, building empires with bronze swords.

Whatever common proto-civilization the blacks brought with them in their retreat from the Sahara, it was naturally altered by the nature of their new environment. For example, the black Africans noted the beauty of tropical bird plumage and began a tradition of using feather-work for ornaments and tokens of authority. This art was entirely unknown in the Mediterranean area but is shared by the high cultures of the New World. It is thus an important culture trait suggesting black African contact with the New World.

There is one African trait, shared with the Americas, that makes it exceedingly difficult to trace black African influence in the New World. Archeological evidence proves that black Africans were there, but we cannot with assurance assess their cultural impact. As Basil Davidson has explained at some length, black Africans conceived of gods as granting the right to settle in, but not own in our Western sense, land under the gods' protection. Therefore, instead of imposing their own gods when they migrated into a new region, black Africans more commonly adopted whatever gods were already worshiped by the existing inhabitants. Davidson relates how one migrant from West Africa, Wene, led his people south into the Congo:

> Wene, chief of the incomers, thereupon married into one of the clans of the people already settled in the area. But the clan he chose was one whose ancestors were recognized as holding spiritual title to the land. . . . He could properly take over [the] title of *mani* and rule as Mani-Kongo, Lord of Congo, duly accepted by the spirit of the earth.[21]

This custom from Africa was carried across the Atlantic by black slaves, and when slaves revolted against their masters and escaped into the American bush, they established similar relations with Amerindians.

> Among the so-called "Bush Negroes" of Surinam—descendants of West Africans taken to this Dutch colony after 1600 who had escaped to the forest and conserved their independence—. . . the spirits of the Earth were regarded as the possession of the original inhabitants, of the "Indians" whose ancestors had first inhabited this land.[22]

This attitude is in marked contrast to that of European cultures. While the black Africans customarily fused with other peoples, and adopted the gods and ancestors of the original inhabitants of any new place, Europeans have dispossessed the original inhabitants of their lands and gods and imposed European gods upon them. At the same time they segregated themselves from the native population in a superior social position. This process is so "natural" to us that we automatically assess cultural influence in terms of imported and imposed gods and customs, in terms of conquest.

Obviously, this method of assessing cultural influence will not work when considering the possible and probable impact of black Africa upon the budding cultures of America. Given black attitudes, we may be confronted with a cultural fusion so subtle as to be unrecognizable. This is a point of utmost importance which must be stressed at somewhat greater length because it permeates our conception of "discovery."

We are fairly certain that both the Irish and the Norse laid eyes on the Americas before Columbus. Some scientists are willing to grant that white men of some more ancient time also "discovered" the New World. And it is written that the Chinese discovered a great land to the east across the Pacific and subsequently sent a massive expedition of colonists to it.

We credit these "discoveries" only grudgingly, just as we are slow to credit the Inca "discovery" of Polynesia. Yet we feel there is something satisfyingly real and solid about the discovery of Columbus. That psychological reality is conquest and exploitation. "Discovery" is not enough.

Doubtless, the Norse and whatever Carthaginians-Phoenicians may have sailed here had the spirit of conquest; they merely lacked the technology of firearms to settle and exploit the new land. It is perhaps symptomatic of our psychology that we accept the Norse discovery and even seem willing to accept an ancient Phoenician presence in the New World, but we also seem a bit hesitant and uneasy about the inconclusiveness of their achievements. We are still exceedingly skeptical about any Irish presence in America before Columbus because we know that the Irish sea-going priests would have ventured forth with a peculiarly Celtic outlook and had not conquest but religious visions in mind. So, in spite of the fact that obviously Celtic ruins positively clutter the landscape of New England, far outnumbering any Norse artifacts found in the New World, we doubt the Irish presence. The Irish never intended to conquer and therefore did not "discover."

How much more, then, will we doubt the achievements and discoveries of peoples whom we have conquered?

It is this prejudice that dictated doubt about Inca sea-going accomplishments, and it will doubtless cause smirks at the thought of black African discovery of the New World—in spite of all concrete evidence. We cannot conceive of discovery without conquest and exploitation. The fusion of peoples, the submergence of individual cultural identities in something completely new, is unthinkable to us.

Yet, I think this is what happened with the black Africans and the Amerindians in the New World. Since there is hard evidence of pre-Colombian blacks in the Americas, but little evidence of massive black African influence, a true fusion must have occurred, a fusion such as we whites have seldom known and may be incapable of perceiving.

3

The Puzzle of Diffusion

Suppose that America had not been discovered by Columbus in 1492 and that, somehow, Europe and the rest of the world had developed today's technology and customs in ignorance of the New World across the Atlantic. Then, in 1980, some intrepid sea captain or jet pilot driven off course sighted the huge unknown continents. The new discovery would be quickly explored, colonized and exploited.

Let us suppose something else equally unlikely—that there had been no progress in American cultures and that Aztecs of the time of Montezuma and Incas of the time of Atahualpa lingered to greet the discoverers on shore. Given the state of international finance these days, it is possible that the gold lust of contemporary English, Spanish, French—and Swiss—discoverers would match that of fifteenth century conquistadors; but let's be charitable and assume that modern democratic and humanist philosophy would dictate trade with these newly discovered people rather than sheer rape of their riches. Cultural diffusion would take place. In return for Mexican and Peruvian gold (and Mexican and Venezuelan oil), the Aztecs and Incas would presumably acquire Volkswagens, microwave ovens, blue jeans and psychotherapy. In imitation of advanced civilization, perhaps, or as the Aztecs and Incas took over their own branch plant management of European multinational corporations, the peoples of Mexico and Peru would begin to build square, glass-sided skyscrapers to house representatives of the supreme deity both they and the Europeans now shared—money.

For a while, until the Aztecs and Incas trained their own audiovisual technicians, they would record the discovery and contact in their traditional art forms. They would make murals and sculptures of the Europeans and their marvelous technological objects as they saw them.

Now, let us suppose something not altogether improbable. Let us imagine that shortly after this discovery and cultural contact, say sometime within the next twenty years, fiscal, political and/or nuclear catastrophe overtakes European and Western civilization. For many generations thereafter there is a "dark age." In the year 2500 A.D., perhaps, some European archeologist again "discovers" the American continent. He will find Aztec murals and Inca statues representing VW Rabbits, microwave ovens and analysts with their patients on couches. Here and there on the landscape will be remains of once tall, square, glass-sided skyscrapers. Excavation in these structures may recover religious artifacts—executive briefcases, golden trophies for salesmanship, the Dior high heels of a few token women management personnel obviously held in high esteem as shown by their unique footwear. The archeologist of the future will likely conclude, rightly, that cultural diffusion between Western Europe and the Americas was accomplished at some time in the latter half of the twentieth century. The archeologist may find a 1970 edition of the *Sayings of Chairman Mao* at some rural site in Nicaragua, Bolivia or Chile. He will conclude, again rightly, that there had also been East Asian cultural contact with the Americas and that the philosophy was, somehow, opposed to the beliefs represented by the monumental skyscrapers in the urban centers. The finding of this booklet will allow the archeologist to pin down the date of contact to the last three or four decades of the present century and allow him to assume ideological conflict and cultural confusion in the Americas. It will also present him with another puzzle of cultural diffusion: how the devil did a Western European named Marx manage to invent a religion that was not widely adopted in his own culture bloc, but was eagerly adopted by the Chinese?

We will leave this future archeologist with his puzzles of diffusion, because our problems are much worse.

In the Americas we are faced with evidence that there was pre-Columbian contact between the Old World and the New. In both the ancient Near East and the Americas, cultures raised pyramids, practiced mummification and trepanning, possessed reed boats of a similar type, shared religious conceptions and domesticated plants. Often, the art is strikingly similar in terms of both motif and execution.

But there is a big problem of chronology. As Thor Heyerdahl

puts it: "The only trouble is that at the time when the great civilizations were beginning to flourish in the New World, some centuries before Christ if present theories hold good, a couple of thousand years had passed since the corresponding culture had ceased to exist in Egypt."[1]

To get this problem in perspective, let us go back to the preposterous scenario of the modern discovery of America. It is as if contemporary ocean freighter captains and multinational corporation executives appeared on American shores as, say, Norman knights. That future archeologist would then share the puzzlement confronting us. He would be fairly certain that cultural contact had taken place between European and American cultures in the twentieth century, but the Aztec murals and Inca sculptures would not show three-piece suits and briefcases, but chain mail and cross-bows; not psychoanalysts and their patients on couches, but medieval priests exorcising demons; no skyscrapers, but ruins of Gothic cathedrals. None of it would make much sense to him, just as none of the evidence for past diffusion makes much sense to our own archeologists.

If present dating theories are accurate, American civilizations began building pyramids of the oldest Egyptian type about 2,000 years after the Egyptians themselves stopped building them. The American civilizations began to work in bronze just when iron was supplanting bronze in the Old World, and there is no evidence that American cultures ever worked iron thereafter. It appears that some American cultures began to use reed ships for ocean passages, along with their own rafts, long after wood had replaced reed for most ocean-going Near Eastern ships.

There seem to be only two possibilities. Either our dating methods are seriously in error and American cultures really began to flourish at the same time as cultures in the ancient Near East, or, somehow, an antique version of Near Eastern culture was brought to American shores and affected the budding of Amerindian civilizations in a way that preserved characteristics long since out-of-date in the Near East itself.

Let us consider the second possibility first. If it is true, then this first cultural infusion or diffusion of outmoded Near Eastern culture was so strong that it dictated the pattern of future development irrespective of later and more advanced cultural input. Although it seems certain that Near Easterners trickled over to the New World at various dates after cultural beginnings in America, and although they would doubtless

American stepped pyramid. *American cultures began raising these stepped pyramids long after the Egyptians had changed to their characteristic smooth-faced type of pyramid.*

have brought more modern ideas of civilization with them, their influence was insufficient to "modernize" American culture. They did not succeed in introducing the use of iron, nor did they succeed in persuading the Amerindians to adopt the new smooth-faced pyramid; instead the Amerindians stayed with their bronze and their stepped pyramids. Although some of these Near Eastern visitors were later remembered as white gods who brought civilized techniques, it seems obvious that their numbers and their cultural offerings were not enough to "update" the ideas adopted from the first cultural infusion.

This is not to deny the contribution to American civilizations of obviously white culture-bearers, but we should try to get some perspective on the magnitude and significance of the contribution. Men from the Mediterranean probably taught American cultures how to work monumentally in stone. But if stonework sometimes replaced the more archaic adobe, the style of American architecture does not reflect that of later Mediterranean building; it retains the older flavor of ancient Near Eastern adobe-work leavened with indigenous and perhaps unidentified foreign concepts. We must also remember that, although we concentrate on the monumental stone architecture of Yucatan and the Andes, most of the population lived in adobe brickwork houses and most buildings were constructed with this material.

Similarly, American religious conceptions show the influence of several "white" philosophies, including primitive Christianity. These were introduced at different times and by different culture-bearers who were later remembered as gods. But these later influences were imposed upon much older concepts: sun-worship that probably came out of Africa, but not necessarily out of Egypt as we know it; and a generalized polytheistic animism that was probably a mixture of indigenous and African beliefs. Most people probably possessed a living religious belief composed of the sun-worship and animistic elements rather than of the later "white-god"-imposed superficialities.

In proposing a black discovery of America, and a black African contribution to American cultural beginnings, I am not denying the evidence of some artifacts and some legends about white culture-bearers. But I am proposing that the black element was introduced earlier and formed, together with native Amerindian conceptions, the basis of American civilization. The white gods came later, and their influences were superimposed upon what already existed. This accounts for the confusing and often contradictory mélange of American culture before Columbus.

One thing is clear. White gods do not solve the puzzle of American civilized beginnings. If Chavin culture, the first American proto-civilization, began about 500 B.C., then white gods from the Near East cannot have been the inspiration for it. The civilization similar to that which began with Chavin ceased to exist in the Near East about 2,000 years earlier.

But the chronological problem of diffusion disappears if we consider West Africa as the primary and earliest culture-source in the Americas. Many West African peoples migrated from the Nile to the Niger in very early times. They brought with them and preserved culture traits and patterns characteristic of pre-dynastic and early dynastic Egypt. Their legacy was never entirely lost. New cultural trends from the Nile and Mesopotamia reached them belatedly because of distance and the barrier of the growing dryness of the Sahara. These people preserved archaic Near East lifestyles, not because they were inherently incapable of progressing on their own, but because the new West African environment they entered presented difficulties that demanded most of their energy for simple survival.

Yet these people did well enough. By 3000 B.C. they were producing portraiture in ceramics and carving crude statues in stone. By 1200 B.C. they were working bronze and precious metals, weaving and dying cotton, building upon religious conceptions current in predynastic Egypt with local African accretions. They built cities with mud-brick and clay architecture of a distinctive style, but not unlike the earliest similar architecture in the foothills of the Andes and in Mexico—or Egypt. But they did not acquire iron until a thousand years after it was in use in the Near East.

The problem of cultural diffusion between the Old World and the New requires, for its primary solution, a source of archaic Egyptian-like proto-civilization somewhere on the Atlantic coast. That source must have knowledge of working bronze and precious metals, but not iron; it must have archaic Egyptian-like architecture in mud-brick and adobe; it must have a knowledge of cotton domestication and weaving; it must have a knowledge of stepped pyramids only, and of reed boats. And it must have all these requirements at about 1000 to 800 B.C.

The only culture that fits this description is the proto-civilization of West Africa.

It would be helpful if the hypothetical culture source in the Old World also knew certain musical instruments like the "pan-pipe," and also had some familiarity with feather-work, which is entirely unknown in the ancient Near East. It would help if its religious ideas were of an extremely ancient type, so ancient that they could have been the foundation of Egyptian religion itself. Finally, of course, such a culture source must have been able to cross the Atlantic at a point where, given the winds and currents, its mariners would be cast up on the American shore and be able to reach the place where American civilization seems to have begun.

Not only is West Africa the single culture that fulfills these conditions, but West Africans would have had by far the shortest Atlantic passage to the New World's first center of civilized beginnings.

So we have established an antique version of Near Eastern civilization that could be the primal source of cultural diffusion from the Old World to the New. But what about the other possibility. What if our dating methods are in error?

Conventional wisdom has it that "a system of relative chronology can be established by excavation in any country that has long been inhabited, but it is left hanging in the air until linked up with Egypt."[2]

H. R. Hall, one of the contributors to the definitive *Cambridge Ancient History*, writes:

> Absolute certainty in these matters [of chronology] is only possible where a continuous literary tradition has always existed. The modern study of European and American prehistoric archeology, for instance, which has no literary tradition by its side, must always remain largely guesswork. The main scheme of the history of ancient Egypt is now a certainty, not a mere hypothesis; but it is very doubtful if it would ever have become a certainty if its construction had depended entirely on the archeologists. The complete skeleton of the scheme was provided by the continuous literary tradition preserved by the Egyptian priest Manetho; this has been clothed with flesh by the archeologists.[3]

Yet, elsewhere in the same work, Hall comments that Manetho's king-list of Egyptian history is "so terribly mangled by copyists that it would be most unsafe to trust its data."[4]

How accurate is our scheme of the history of ancient Egypt? Since 1950, Immanuel Velikovsky has argued that the main scheme of Egyptian history is anything but a certainty and that the chronology of the ancient world that scholars have built upon it is therefore unreliable. Velikovsky believes that a natural upheaval occurred about 1500 B.C. that resulted in the subsequent history of Egypt becoming confused. Comparing documents on a generation-by-generation basis, Velikovsky matched the history of Egypt against the histories of Greece, Israel, Assyria, Babylonia and Persia from roughly 1400 B.C. until about 330 B.C. when Alexander of Macedon came to Egypt. He concluded that the history of Egypt is some 600 to 800 years too long, that some supposed "dynasties" never existed, some ruled concurrently, and others have been duplicated. Velikovsky also argues that modern archeologists arrived at "certain" dates of some Egyptian rulers using dubious astronomical assumptions and laboring under misconceptions about astronomy.

Velikovsky postulates that a natural catastrophe increased the carbon-hydrogen content of the atmosphere, the ground and all organic substances. Therefore, C14 dating, which is based on present levels of carbon concentration, is inaccurate.

In spite of howls from the knowledge establishment, Velikovsky has a point. C14 dates after about 1400 to 1200 B.C. are known to be accurate when related to our present atmospheric carbon levels; but they have been proved to be wildly inaccurate for dates before about 1400 B.C. when compared to the annual growth rings of long-lived trees, such as the bristlecone pines of California, which may live to an age of 8,000 years. Radiocarbon dates before 1400 to 1200 B.C. must be calibrated, that is, "corrected," according to the chronology offered by the analysis of annual growth rings of trees.

Velikovsky's reconstruction of ancient history was given dramatic support by King Tutankhamen's burial goods, which were exhibited in major Western cities recently. Conventional chronology says that King Tut died about 1350 B.C.; Velikovsky's reconstruction of ancient history has Tutankhamen entombed no earlier than about 850 B.C. Five hundred years difference. In order to settle the issue, Velikovsky tried for ten years to have some pieces of King Tut's treasure released for C14 dating. Finally, in 1971, a few pieces of wood and reed mat were analyzed by the University of Pennsylvania's radiocarbon laboratory; the results indicated that the reed for the mats had been picked in 846 B.C.[5]

Needless to say, the University of Pennsylvania did not make public this astounding result. For if Velikovsky's reconstruction of ancient history is correct, conventional chronology is a shambles, and one more modern scientific myth. Our pattern of ancient history is a farce.

For, if Velikovsky is correct in his revised chronology, the entire period of ancient history becomes 600 to 800 years too long. Some events and empires become figments of modern scientific imagination. Velikovsky claims there was no Greek dark age from 1200 until 800 B.C., there was no Hittite Empire; the mysterious "peoples of the sea" whom Rameses III supposedly defeated in about 1200 B.C. are, in fact, Greeks and Persians of the Classical period, and we know the names of their commanders.

Naturally, professional academics do not look kindly on Velikovsky. One Egyptologist told me that "Velikovsky looked at only ten per cent of the evidence, and ignored the other ninety per cent in order to reach his conclusions." Other representatives of academia have not hesitated to brand him an outright liar and charlatan. Velikovsky's original publisher was threatened by professors and universities who warned that if Velikovsky's books were published there would be a boycott of the publisher's standard textbooks! So much for modern tolerance.

After several years of study, I have become convinced of what Velikovsky himself asserted: that his reconstruction of ancient historical chronology contradicts no facts but only the interpretation of those facts by modern experts. These interpretations have been repeated so often that they have come to be regarded as fact and are taught as fact, but they remain only interpretations.

Assuming, then, that Velikovsky's chronology is correct, the predynastic period and the early dynastic period of Egyptian history must be moved forward—600 to 800 years nearer to our own time and to the beginnings of civilization in America by the same count of years. The chronology gap narrows considerably, but it still leaves us with a "cultural gap" of at least a thousand years.

Using Velikovsky's chronology, it becomes barely possible that Egyptians and Phoenicians brought an archaic version of Near Eastern culture to the Americas; however there is still support, not only for an independent black discovery of America, but for supposing that this black discovery was the first and most influential one. The only thing that really changes is that it is possible to believe that not long after the black discovery, perhaps only a generation or two after it, Egyptians and Phoenicians may have sailed directly to the New World. Even so, murals at Chichen Itza testify that when white men arrived, blacks were already established in the New World.

The combination of our two conditions solves the puzzle of the supposed anomalies of diffusion. Velikovsky's revised chronology, together with the consideration of a West African cultural contact with America, allows the pieces to fall into place. The resulting picture may challenge the myths and prejudices of our time, but does no violence to the facts or to the cohesion of history.

4

Olman

I have found that most of us with any pretentions to a general knowledge of history have a pretty good idea of the broader trends of European history, and some vague idea of the major events of Asiatic history. We may have some notion of African history, though this peters out after the "Egyptians" and picks up again with Stanley and Livingstone, some hazy ideas about the Incas, and even some mostly romantic conceptions of the Polynesians tenuously grounded in fact and John Wayne movies.

Where almost everyone simply shrugs, however, is in the pre-Columbian history of Mexico. Beyond a general consensus that the Aztecs were in control of things when the Spanish came, almost everyone draws a complete blank. Some may venture the opinion that Montezuma was king of the Aztecs when Cortés (or was it Pizarro?) waded ashore; but few would dare say more. Even in this lucky guess we are prompted by the "halls of Montezuma" of Marine Corps anthem fame and by travel packages to the lands of "Montezuma's revenge," which seem to be anywhere south of Miami.

I think that, more than anything else, this historical void is due to what I can only call *tec*nicalities. There are altogether too many "tecs" in Mexican history. We have Mixtecs, Aztecs, Zapotecs and Olmecs, not to mention Huaxtecs and Toltecs. The only bright spot in this welter of *tec*nicalities is the Mayas, and I'm convinced that the reason so many popular writers have paid attention to them is simply because the Mayas had the good sense to have given themselves a non-*tec*nical name.

The problem has not been helped much by English literature. How many generations of high school and college students have had to read nonsense like "And stout Cortés, with all his men . . . Silent, upon a peak in Darien"? Of course, Cortés never stood silent in Darien, nor did he view the Pacific Ocean with "wild surmise" or any other emotion for that matter. Cortés

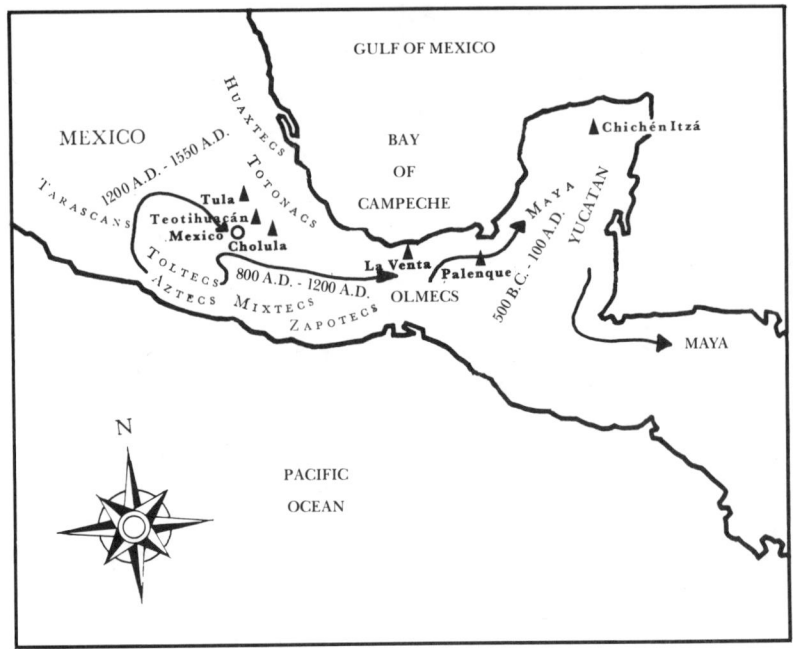

Meso-America

In general terms, Meso-American high civilization seems to have begun with the Olmecs, who lived in the coastal areas of the Bay of Campeche from perhaps 500 B.C. until the first years of the present era. Olmec culture then passed to the Mayas of Yucatan, where a distinctive civilization flourished from the first Christian years until about 1200 A.D. Thereafter, inland tribes such as the Toltecs and the Aztecs became dominant, taking over Mayan culture, adapting it and modifying it both in Yucatan and in Mexico.

By the time the Spanish arrived, the Aztecs were rulers over much of Mexico, but the Mayas still lived independently in parts of Yucatan and farther south in Central America. Meso-American traditions seem to indicate that there were two distinct cultural thrusts: an imported culture in Yucatan and around the Bay of Campeche; and a native culture center inland in the Valley of Mexico. These two traditions began to merge about 100 A.D., and resulted in the Mexican/Aztec civilization that confronted Cortés and the Spanish.

never saw the Pacific Ocean at all.

But such is history. Between the "tecs" and the distortions of English Lit, most people just throw up their hands and give up on what happened in Mexico before Columbus. Not only are the various conquered peoples muddled in popular knowledge, but—very strange for Westerners—the conquerers are almost equally confused. The Mexican ruins left for tourists to see were built by Aztecs . . . Olmecs? . . . Toltecs? . . . well, whoever. And it was Cortés . . . Balboa? . . . Pizarro? . . . well, whoever, who defeated Montezuma.

Thank goodness we can always fall back on the Mayas. No "tecs" these Mayas, and they even stayed put in Yucatan, more or less.

Herewith, and with apologies to people like Dr. H. D. Disselhoff, director of the Ethnological Museum in Berlin, and his predecessor, Dr. Walter Krickeberg, "doyen and leading expert in the field of American studies," I present my understanding of Mexican history before Cortés. In the unlikely event that colleagues of Disselhoff and Krickeberg will ever chance to read what follows, I am sure that their verdict would be that it amounts to distortive oversimplification. On the other hand, in self-defense, I will mention that one of these two esteemed gentlemen—either Disselhoff or Krickeberg—is probably responsible for the error of confidently labeling *guara* boards as "agricultural implements" among the displays of this acclaimed Ethnological Museum in Berlin and, in committing this seemingly trifling mistake, contributed mightily to everybody believing that the Polynesians came into the Pacific from the west, and bucked thousands of miles of contrary currents and winds. This view has inspired any number of textbooks that are now so much rubbish and wasted pulpwood. I doubt that any errors of omission and oversimplification made below will prove to be as serious.

An understanding of Mexican history is easy, providing one has a reasonable grasp on our own European story. If we talked to a reasonably bright Englishman or Frenchman today we would be told that once all of the existing European nations were barbarians and that they cooperated in destroying the civilization of Rome. Further, we would be told that before Rome there was an earlier civilization in Greece from which the Romans themselves had borrowed much. Then, there was a vague and slightly foreign-seeming civilization across the Mediterranean in Egypt which, they would guess, might have started the whole civilized ball of wax. We would also be informed that, since the fall of Rome about 2,000 years ago, these barbarian nations not only evolved slowly and painfully toward "civilization," but also continually fought among themselves so that first one nation would be dominant in Europe, and then another, as fortunes shifted.

If we seemed inclined to doubt that the English or French cultures of the last century really had much to do with Rome, our Englishman might drag us through the streets of London and point out all the buildings with Roman architecture. He may admit that there was no English alphabet and that the barbarous Angles, Saxons, Jutes and Normans had merely borrowed the Roman alphabet. He might coax us into an art gallery and point out the Victorian paintings of Alma-Tadema, the best-selling painter of the 1870s, which depict ancient Greeks and Romans—but mostly female ones—draped or bathing, or picnicking, or flirting amid lustrous columns and balustrades of marble. Indeed, Alma-Tadema stuck to this theme so consistently that *Punch* was forced to concede that he was "a marbellous painter."

A Frenchman would say much the same thing, though possibly stressing that as France was happily located nearer to the source of this ancient Roman culture, it was understandable that French civilization has always been a bit more advanced when compared with, say, the English. Our Frenchman could show us the same sort of architecture, make the same admission about the alphabet, and find lithographs as ghastly as the work of Tadema, showing Napoleon's Empress Josephine lounging about in fake "classical" dress.

French and English might unite to point figuratively across the Atlantic to remind us that even the Capitol building in Washington was inspired by Roman architecture, and that buildings symbolizing the very foundation of American society—any number of First National Banks—recall architecture in the Eternal City.

Faced with all this "evidence," we may concede that all the jostling European powers, and even their transatlantic social offspring, could trace much of their culture back to Rome. Granting that the Romans took much from the Greeks, who took something very vague from the Egyptians, Western history is perceived to have some continuity stretching back several thousand years.

Mexico is no different.

Think of the Aztecs as the English, and the Toltecs as the French—or vice versa. When Cortés landed on Mexican shores in 1519, the Aztecs had gained the upper hand through a combination of outright conquest of some peoples, intimidation of many more, and merely token suzerainty over others—much like, say, Napoleon's empire in Europe from 1803 to about 1812. Previously the Toltecs had had the upper hand. The Zapotecs, Huaxtecs, Mixtecs, etc. can be regarded as Germans,

Swedes and Danes. They moved around within Mexico and may have had brief periods of dominance; but they did not manage to put together empires comparable to those of the Toltecs and, later, the Aztecs.

Being neighbors, the peoples of Mexico naturally merged and mingled quite a bit, just as the Europeans did; but the Mexican peoples still preserved some aspects of distinctiveness. Most had their own languages, though these were as closely related as European ones. They stressed different aspects of what seems to have been generally similar religious conceptions. Just as German Protestantism differs a bit from Anglicanism and both differ a bit from Catholicism and as Judaism differs somewhat from all, they clearly all come from much the same tradition. Just as the English population is a composite of many formerly distinct peoples, so the Aztecs were an amalgamation of tribes of former barbarian tribes from the northwest part of Mexico. So also were the Toltecs.

Within this analogy, the Old Mayan culture in Yucatan flourishing from perhaps 100 B.C. until 800 A.D. or so becomes our Mexican "Rome."[2] The later Mayan "New Empire" and Chichen Itza phases correspond to the medieval Italian city-states: they occupied the same space as the former Romans, but were different because of intermarriage with various invaders. The later Mayans present exactly the same circumstance as the later Italians, and for the same reason. Maya country was invaded by people from the north (just as Italy was) and the resulting composite population developed a culture that was different from the Old Maya Empire—"Rome"—and had its own characteristics like Italy in the Renaissance and today.

About the only historical problem with this analogy is that the later Mayas were much better fighters than, say, modern Italians. Francisco de Montejo occupied the Mayan capital in 1533, but it took him thirteen years of bloody warfare to conquer Yucatan alone. The last Mayan city, Tayasal, did not fall to the Spanish until 1687.

If the Old Mayas are our Mexican Romans, then the Olmecs become our Mexican "Greeks." Their culture seems to have started things along the lines that could be called "Mexican," and Cortés would eventually meet it after about two thousand years of development.

This completes our analogy and, I hope, makes the *tec*nicalities a bit less confusing. The Aztecs or Toltecs can be compared to the English and the French; Zapotecs, Huaxtecs, Mixtecs, Tarascans and all the other "tecs" can be thought of as Swedes, Danes, Germans and Belgians; the Old Mayans are our ancient Romans, the New Mayans our Renaissance Italians; the Olmecs become the oldest characteristically Mexican culture source, just as we presume to trace our characteristic Western culture back to the Greeks.

Later Mexican Indian chroniclers remembered the Land of Olman as a paradise populated by especially gifted people. Cocoa and rubber grew in abundance and the people wove beautiful garments from the brilliant plumage of gorgeous tropical birds. All the great advances of civilization had originally been made in Olman. The people, so it was said, had worshiped goddesses of earth and moon. They made ornaments of hardest jade and metal with apparent ease.

European scholars were inclined to dismiss the stories of Olman as mere myth and legend. But while on the coast of the Gulf of Mexico in 1884, Alfredo Chavero found carved stone heads of incredible proportions and a number of axe-heads with human faces and figures carved onto them. None of this art showed much affinity with known Mexican motifs. Then, later researchers in the same area found characteristic figurines—a mixture of jaguar and man—of some lost, unknown and unsuspected culture.

Rumors of the giant stone heads eventually reached archeologists, and in 1938 Matthew W. Stirling of the National Geographic Society found and photographed a giant stone head near the village of Tres Zapotes.

Full-scale excavation began on January 1, 1939, and very shortly Stirling and Dr. C. W. Weiant looked upon the strange statue. It was six feet in diameter and carved very naturalistically. "It is incredibly lifelike, strikingly dissimilar to any other American Indian sculpture that I had seen."[1] It appeared to be a gigantic portrait of a black man, because there was no doubt that the features were Negroid. Several more such heads have subsequently been found, the largest about ten feet in diameter and weighing an estimated thirty tons. All revealed Negroid features and all depicted a sort of unadorned football helmet. Most were found at the village of La Venta, a few miles from Tres Zapotes.

Archeologists have gone out of their way to avoid calling

One of several giant stone heads *found at La Venta and Tres Zapotes on Mexico's Caribbean coast that show negroid features and characteristic "football helmet."*

these heads Negroid. The usual terminology is "baby face," and there is much reference to "infantile features" and "thick lips." But popular writers have not been afraid to admit the Negro features, although some of them, being obsessed with finding evidence pertaining to white gods have sometimes been uncertain as to the proper way of treating this collection of obviously Negro sculpture. Pierre Honoré is of this sort of troubled popular writer and he becomes almost as coy as the archeologists with their "baby faces" when he writes in *In Quest of the White God*:

> The statues do not represent Indians. Though they are of men who have many features in common, pointing to one particular race, it is not the Indian one; and these men wear

helmets with flaps protecting the cheeks.... The White God wore a helmet.

"Pointing to one particular race" indeed! So they do, these statues, but not one offering a likely candidate for a white god!

On January 16, 1939, Stirling's workmen uncovered a fragment of a large stela carved in low relief: "Peering close, I saw that a beautifully carved row of bars and dots ran across the stone.... These immediately suggested a Maya calendar date, something we had all hoped for but had not dared to expect."[2] Copying the characters, Stirling ran for camp and his reference sources. The date was 6 Eznab 1 Uo in Mayan, which the glyphs resembled but did not exactly duplicate. This works out to November 4, 291 B.C., and is the oldest known date inscribed on a New World artifact.

As early as 1925, Frans Blom had photographed the top of another giant head near La Venta. Blom had had no time to excavate, but Stirling was in no doubt that the bowl-shaped object in the Blom photograph could only be the crown of another "baby face" statue. Accordingly, Stirling and his colleagues abandoned Tres Zapotes when the site had been excavated to a depth of twenty feet and moved on to La Venta. Almost immediately a "city" and a pyramid were discovered. The pyramid was not of stone but was a huge earth mound 105 feet high and about 100 yards square on the base; pillars of one or more ruined temples indicated a social center of some sort.

Excavation revealed a number of small figurines, toys with wheels, and yet more giant heads. Perhaps the most dramatic find was a polished stone mosaic that had once adorned the pavement of a plaza. This was in the likeness of a jaguar.

Besides Tres Zapotes and La Venta, several other sites with similar artifacts have been located over the years. Stirling related this culture to the legendary coastal land of Olman, and accordingly called it Olmec:

> Olmec culture began before 1000 B.C. and reached its peak between 800 and 500 B.C. In the jungles of Vera Cruz and Tabasco they erected ceremonial centres that flourished before the rise of Maya, Zapotec, Toltec and Totonac cultures. The great earth mounds that loomed from hot leafy jungles were precursors to the soaring stone pyramids of the Maya and the Aztecs.[3]

The early dates found by Stirling on Olmec monuments "suggest that these Olmec people originated the marvelous calendar that subsequently gave the Maya their supreme claim to intellectual fame."[4] Stirling concludes that these Olmecs gave "to ancient Mexico its first great cultural impetus."

Apparently, these Olmecs possessed a hieroglyphic system of writing similar to that later used by the Mayas. The conclusion must be that the Mayas adapted the Olmec glyphs. Stirling excavated the cover of "an ancient illustrated volume" at Cerro de las Mesas, but "its pages had entirely disappeared"[5] so it is not known what this writing system may have been in its early form. This is a great pity because such a book might have been most helpful in our attempts to decipher Mayan. At present we can read little more than dates.

So much for the Olmecs or "La Venta Man." Little more is known about them. Their cultural influence seems to have spread from the coast as far inland as Monte Alban and Mitla where curiously Negroid figures and faces appear in early Mixtec and Zapotec reliefs. Later, much of Olmec culture passed on, obviously, to the Mayas.

No one has any meaningful answer to the problem of who these Olmecs were. Stirling's original excavations, and later ones, seem to indicate that there was an original and completely "native" culture existing along the coastline of the Bay of Campeche as early as 1000 B.C. These people were not yet Olmecs and their culture, a relatively basic one, seems to have been part of a pan-Mexican culture flourishing in many places and having some sort of relationship with South American Chavin.[6]

Around 500 B.C., if not a little before, someone else arrived in the Bay of Campeche and fused with the local culture. The result was both Olmec and also distinctively different from the basic pan-Mexican culture that previously existed in the coastal area and continued to exist beyond Olmec influence. Shortly after 500 B.C., the fused cultures, now Olmec, began to raise mound-pyramids and to carve Negro-featured sculptures from rock. Literally hundreds of finely worked jade "man-jaguar" figurines have been discovered. We have no idea of what this apparently religious or philosophical structure was really like; but aside from the evidence of the Negroid heads, one *can* say that something very similar is known from West Africa. There, instead of "jaguar societies," we have "leopard

societies" whose importance and significance is still not well understood by anyone except the black Africans themselves. But we do know that a man/cat motif may be linked with the black African civilization of Kush, because we find representations of lion-headed gods in relief within Kushite temples of about 800 B.C.

It is at least possible that the "jaguar complex" of religious and philosophical thought originated in West Africa and was transplanted to America. The Kushites conceived of a lion-headed but otherwise human god of some sort. But there are no lions in the forested areas of West Africa; there the leopard takes the place of the lion as the largest predatory cat. If Kushite beliefs trickled into West Africa, or were brought there wholesale by migration, it is reasonable that the man/cat belief structure might have been transferred from the lion to the leopard.

If this cultural trait migrated to America, yet another transfer of attributes would be needed. For there are no leopards in the New World. The jaguar, however, makes an excellent substitute, having the same general markings and coloration as a leopard. In fact, West African Akan statues of leopards look remarkably similar to some New World jaguar renditions—particularly

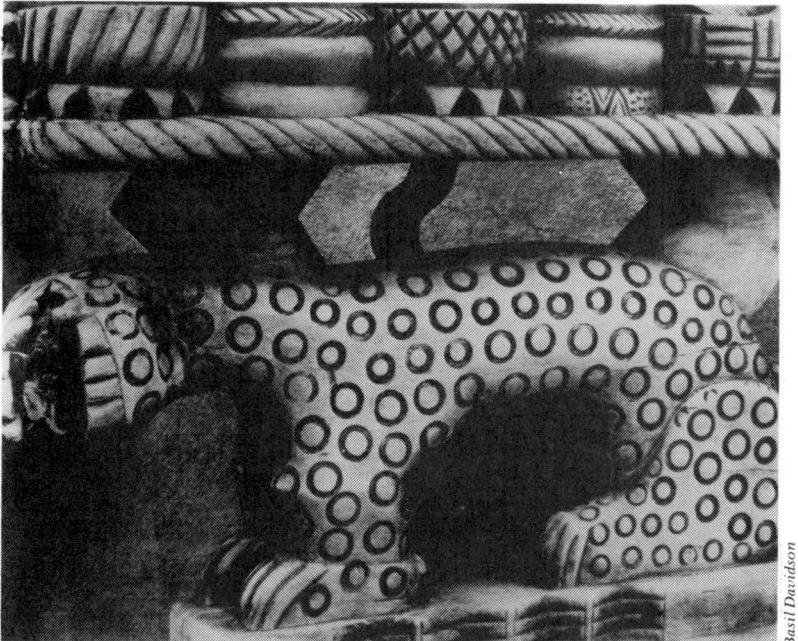

The famous jaguar throne from Chichen Itza *(left)* **and West African chief's throne** *share a stylistic treatment of the feline motif. Note that the heads are even turned in the same direction, and the mouths are open and treated similarly. The representation of the feet and spots are almost identical.*

the so-called "jaguar throne" of the Temple of Kukulcan in Chichen Itza.[7]

At any rate, I think that the conceptual parallel between the "jaguar society" of the Olmecs and the "leopard societies" of West Africans is at least as significant and suggestive as more material parallels, such as pottery types and reed boats, often cited by those wishing to support the notion of transoceanic cultural contact.

One thing is certain. Olmec culture began to differentiate itself from the pan-Mexican basic culture just when Negroes may be assumed, on the evidence of the giant sculpted heads, to have landed on the coast of the Bay of Campeche. The Olmec jaguar-man concept suddenly appeared at the same time and who but West Africans were more likely to bring such an idea? It is at least a reasonable possibility that this concept may be traced back to Kush because, about this time, the Kushites were reeling away in all directions under the iron weapons of Assyria,

Relief of the lion god at Naga, *in the ancient African kingdom of Kush. Note the woven cloth tunic. Did Kushite refugees bring their lion-man religious conceptions to West Africa? There, was the leopard substituted for the lion? Later, did West Africans influence the development of the jaguar cults in Mexico?*

and it is known with certainty that some Kushites migrated westward after 600 B.C.

Which brings us to the Mayas.

Sometime just before, or just after, the Christian era began in the Old World, the Mayas "began" in the northern part of Guatemala and gradually moved into the peninsula of Yucatan. There were, of course, people already living in Yucatan and using pottery before the Mayas arrived, but the Mayas adopted this sort of indigenous pottery instead of bringing their own presumably more advanced and civilized styles. As someone once said, these native people of Yucatan "may have spoken Mayan . . . but certainly did not have Mayan culture. They had no stone architecture, no calendar and no hieroglyphic writing and no typical Old Empire pottery." But typical Old Empire pottery seems to have been merely an evolved version of native Yucatan pottery styles.

Which leads us to wonder exactly what Mayan culture really was and where it came from. It seems that, just as on the Bay of Campeche with the Olmecs, there was an infusion of culture from somewhere south of Yucatan, on the Gulf of Honduras, which resulted in some Mayan-speakers suddenly acquiring what we call Mayan culture. However they got this culture, they carried it into the southeast coast area of Yucatan.

The Mayan Old Empire is usually dated from about 100 A.D. or a bit later until roughly 800 A.D. During this time, many cities of stone were built in Guatemala and present-day Belize and in Yucatan, and all this activity hints that the population in Mayan times was much larger than the million or so people who live in this area today. A study of present-day Mayan agricultural techniques, which seem to be very archaic and probably essentially unchanged from those of the Old Empire, has shown Mayan agriculture could support many more people than today's population of Yucatan and nearby Mayan sites. A contemporary Mayan man can support a family of five by working in his cornfields only sixty days per year. It is reasonable to assume, then, that there were enough people in the region to raise all the stone cities.

These were not really cities in our current sense. They were not concentrations of population, but ceremonial centers inhabited for most of the year only by priests and perhaps other favored classes. The great Mayan cities would have been mostly empty, as the bulk of the population lived in scattered villages. The Mayan economy was not sophisticated, and the cities were not centers of commerce with an attendant complex division of labor. Most of the people lived on a simplified village subsistence level.

The Mayans are chiefly known popularly for the accuracy of their calendar which, as everyone knows, was more accurate than European calendars of the sixteenth century. This is true, more or less, except that the Mayan method of time reckoning was also a good deal more cumbersome than the European system. Many writers have cited the great accuracy of Mayan calendars and astronomy as evidence of some cultural infusion from the Old World in ancient times. Such infusion may have occurred, although which Mediterranean people could boast such accuracy to "infuse" remains a mystery. Moreover, the Mayan calendar really bears very little resemblance to any time-reckoning system anywhere else.

"They figured time in *baktuns* (144,000 days), *katuns* (7,200 days), *tuns* (360 days), *uinals* (20 days) and *kins* (1 day)."[8] The earliest known Mayan dated monument reads, in transcription: 8.14.10.13.15 (8 *baktuns*, 14 *katuns*, 10 *tuns*, 13 *uinals* and 15 *kins*). All this is figured from a "beginning" date about 5,000 years ago; this date therefore works out to 68 A.D.

The Mayans had a hieroglyphic writing system, but we cannot read much of it except dates. The individual glyphs themselves bear some similarity to Olmec date glyphs, but do not look anything like other known hieroglyphic writing systems, and least of all like the Egyptian one.

This is certainly not the place to go into all the Mayan mysteries, but one mystery needs to be solved. The only thing that concerns us here are some interesting murals in the Temple of Warriors located in the Mayan city of Chichen Itza. Unfortunately, like everything else concerned with the Mayas, even this limited interest proves to be complicated.

Although Chichen Itza was apparently founded about 500 A.D., its chief period of glory occurred about 400 years later. The Toltecs invaded Mayan land and many new buildings were raised in Chichen Itza by the invaders. One of these was the Temple of Warriors in Chichen Itza, which was evidently dedicated to Quetzalcoatl/Kukulcan. Unfortunately, scholars have ignored the significance of the building itself, and particularly the murals in it, in favor of speculating about the identity of Quetzalcoatl/Kukulcan. As such speculation dominates much of the writing concerning Mexico and Yucatan, a small digression about this "feathered serpent" is in order. There will be a more lengthy discussion of the true significance of Quetzalcoatl/Kukulcan in Chapter Nine.

Aztecs, Toltecs and probably other *"tecs"* held Quetzalcoatl in high regard. (The Mayas knew Quetzalcoatl as "Kukulcan" in their own language.) Quetzalcoatl and Kukulcan are two names for the same belief complex of "man-serpent-quetzal bird-supreme deity-king." We don't know much about Quetzalcoatl/Kukulcan except that "it" was an idea or god depicted in numerous sculptures as a huge feathered serpent, often with a man's face visible within the serpent's open mouth. Beginning about the year 1000 A.D. under the Toltec invaders, this Quetzalcoatl/Kukulcan became suddenly something of a supreme deity in the city of Chichen Itza. Somehow, Quetzalcoatl/Kukulcan is connected with rain and rain-making. To make matters worse, although our Quetzalcoatl/Kukulcan was originally a "god" (for the lack of a better word), the name and idea was appropriated as a personal title by a white Toltec king who established himself in Chichen Itza around 900 to 1000 A.D. Furthermore, it seems that an old, bearded white man once came to the area in very ancient times and, because of his wisdom and kindness, was associated in legend with Quetzalcoatl/Kukulcan.

These complexities will be discussed later (see Chapter Nine); but, confusing as it all is, this is not our present problem with Quetzalcoatl/Kukulcan. Very simply, our question is this: was Quetzalcoatl brought to Chichen Itza as something completely new by Toltecs, or was the idea known previously to the Mayas—a concept dating from Mayan beginnings?

The second possibility seems more likely because the Mayas had their own name—Kukulcan—for the idea/god and did not adopt the invaders' name. It is even possible that Kukulcan had been known by the Mayas from very early times and that they had passed the concept on to interior peoples. Eventually it came back to Mayan land with the Toltecs and enjoyed a dominance at Chichen Itza that it had never possessed under the Mayas themselves.

No one knows for certain whether the Maya Kukulcan was worshiped before the Toltec Quetzalcoatl came to Chichen Itza, but one fact does suggest that Quetzalcoatl/Kukulcan was originally a Mayan conception. The quetzal bird, which gives Quetzalcoatl part of its name, is restricted to the highland part of the old Mayan country and does not, and never did, inhabit the interior of central Mexico where the Aztecs and Toltecs began their rise to power. Although the Mayas, Aztecs and

Toltecs alike apparently worshiped the quetzal from early times, and although all three peoples prized the bird's long iridescent-green tail feathers, the quetzal's natural habitat is in the uplands of Guatemala and Peten. The Aztecs and Toltecs could have only obtained the knowledge—and the feathers—of the bird by prior contact with Mayas. In fact, the Mayas were enriched by their trade in quetzal feathers.[9]

Thus, zoology indicates that "Quetzalcoatl" likely originated with the Mayas, who passed on the concept to the Toltecs and Aztecs. It is merely an irony that the Mayan Kukulcan never achieved the importance of Quetzalcoatl in its own homeland until imposed upon a Mayan city by Toltec invaders.

Aside from whether the "feathered serpent" was known to the Mayas before the Toltecs came, we are also concerned about what buildings existed in Chichen Itza before the Toltecs came. A lot of new buildings rose in Chichen Itza around 1000 A.D. when the Toltecs came: the Tlachtli-ground (ball court); the Temple of Jaguars; the Temple of the Tables; the Caracol, a domed observatory. Unfortunately, no one knows whether the Temple of Warriors dates from this Toltec invasion or earlier. The Temple of Warriors "is the most imposing structure excavated at Chichen Itza," but no one knows the date of the building.

The Temple of Warriors has murals that show warriors of three races: American Indians, white men with blond hair, and black Africans. The black warriors are obviously established among the American Indians because blacks are shown assisting in the sacrifice of captured and defeated whites. Obviously, by the time the battle with the white invaders took place, the blacks were already an important enough part of the "system" that they were permitted to carry out the sacrifice of prisoners. The conclusion must be that the blacks were solidly enfranchised in the native Mayan society when whites were newcomers, invaders, aliens.

We do not know, however, when these murals were painted, or whether the scenes represented a contemporary event, or a past event, to the creators. We do not know if this history was contemporary with the artist, or if it represents an event that took place in remote antiquity.

As Heyerdahl notes, many people have speculated upon the identity of the white warriors pictured in the murals of Chichen Itza. To my knowledge, however, no one has spent much imagination speculating on the identity of the black warriors,

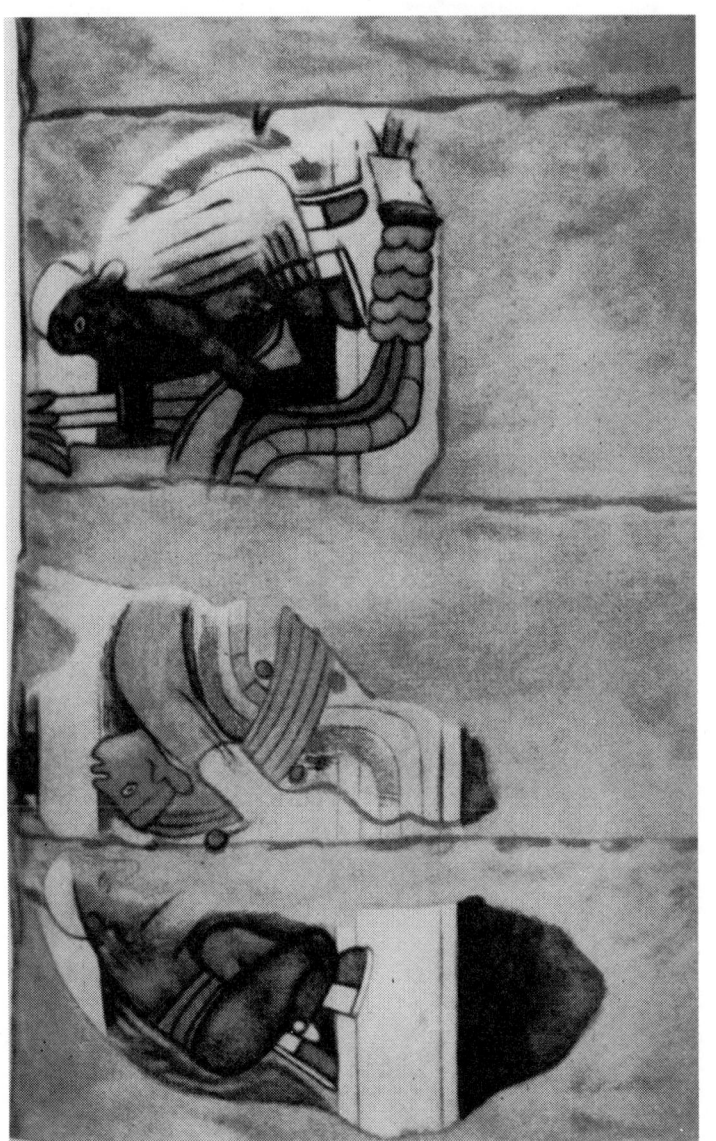

Murals in the Temple of Warriors at Chichen Itza show black and Indian allies in battle against white invaders. Here, a white warrior is being sacrificed by two black warriors. (The center of the scene is damaged.)

Thor Heyerdahl

Color reproductions of these murals clearly show three races (see American Indians in the Pacific by Thor Heyerdahl). Here black warriors march off their captives (left). The murals show the ship of the defeated white warriors (right). Is this a skin boat or did the artist merely neglect to show the planking?

Thor Heyerdahl

nor has there been much speculation about the self-evident fact, insisted upon in the action of the murals themselves, that these black warriors were integrated into Mayan society before the whites came.

To me, the identity of the white warriors seems to be obvious. These whites have blond hair, are shown fighting naked, and have jewelry in their hair. Since we believe that the Yucatan complex began about 500 B.C., they are obviously pre-Christian. The only known white people of that time who had blond hair and who customarily fought naked were the Celts of Iberia and northwest Europe. These warriors can therefore only be Celts. The green stones depicted in the blond hair of these white warriors may also hint at their identity, for Celts are known to have adorned themselves with hair-jewelry. Moreover, the whites' boat in the background seems to be a skin boat; at all events, no hint of planking is shown. The Celtic peoples alone made extensive use of skin vessels from 500 B.C. onwards. As the Celts fought naked only up until late Roman times, the murals at Chichen Itza most probably show a confrontation that took place between 800 B.C. and, say, 300 A.D. at the very latest.

If the battle shown in these murals did, in fact, take place sometime between 800 B.C. and the beginning of the Christian era, then we must assume that the blacks pictured as allies in these scenes had come across the Atlantic earlier yet. They are enfranchised in the local sacrifice-system and wear the same sort of clothing as the American Indian warriors.

We may recall, however, that the Mayan Old Empire itself is generally dated as beginning only about 100 B.C. at the earliest. Therefore, the scenes of the murals show an event that very probably pre-dates the Mayan culture itself. It may even be part of events that began Mayan culture.

Our brief survey of both Olmec and Mayan civilizations reveals that both these highly influential "founding peoples" of Meso-American culture show indisputable evidence of black African contact at the earliest time. There are the Olmec heads with Negroid faces; there are the Mayan murals of black warriors allied to native ones, and blacks conducting ritual sacrifice upon native altars. There are spiritual similarities as well—the suggestive evidence of the links between the jaguar cult of the Olmecs and the leopard societies of West Africa. And, in Chapter Nine, zoological evidence for an African origin of Quetzalcoatl/Kukulcan will be presented.

Before leaving Meso-America, some continuity should be established up to the time of Cortés. As we have seen, the Toltecs grew dominant in the inland areas around Mexico City by about 800 A.D. A couple of hundred years later they were powerful enough to invade Yucatan and to influence Mayan culture at Chichen Itza. Some of the Mayas seem to have fled the Toltec invasion and moved south, back into the border areas of Guatemala from where they originally came. However, in Yucatan itself, the foreign Toltecs were finally defeated by Tutul Xiu, and the Mayan victors established a new capital called Mani ("It is finished"). This name possibly refers to the end of Toltec domination. The composite Toltec-Mayan population of Chichen Itza fell back to the old city of Tayasal, also near the border where present-day Yucatan, Guatemala and British Honduras meet. (These, the last independent Mayas, were finally defeated by Martin de Ursua y Arizmendi, the Spanish governor of Yucatan.)

By the time the Toltecs were finally defeated in Yucatan, a new power had arisen in inland Mexico. A poor but warlike confederacy of tribes—the Aztecs—arrived in the Valley of Mexico and proceeded to duplicate the Toltec rise to power. By about 1200 A.D., the Aztecs challenged the power of the Toltecs themselves. In fact, the two-front war waged by the Toltecs against the Mayas in Yucatan and the Aztecs in the interior very possibly explains the Toltec defeat and Mayan and Aztec victory.

Thus, when Cortés landed in 1519, the Aztecs controlled Mexico and constituted the greatest single source of opposition to the Spanish. Further south, in Guatemala, the Mayans remained independent of both Aztecs and Spaniards for many years.

Olmecs and Mayas were the founding peoples of civilized Meso-America. Other Mexican peoples were inspired by them, and borrowed from them. Before the Land of Olman came into existence on the shores of the Bay of Campeche there was only a primitive "pan-Mexican" culture-complex. Yet it seems that even this pan-Mexican cultural base had apparently been exposed to outside influences. (For example, Disselhoff's analysis of Mexican pottery styles convinced him that there was a "startling affinity" with pottery styles of the Chavin culture of ancient Peru.)

If we have discovered a Negro presence at the very beginning of characteristic Meso-American civilization, is it possible that even older levels of American culture bear traces of black African contact? It is time to turn our attention southward to the eastern slopes of the Andes, to the Chavin proto-civilization and the Muisca cultural complex that preceded it.

5

Green Hell?

Before he lost respectability in the scientific community, the late Ivan T. Sanderson was not only a leading academic and field zoologist with numerous discoveries of importance to his credit, he was also a best-selling popular author and leader of two major scientific and animal-collecting trips to the tropics. He was in Africa in 1933-34 and in South America in 1938, and he lived deep in the interior on both occasions. One of Sanderson's accomplishments was, more or less, the invention of the science of phytozoology, or the distribution of plants and animals in relation to each other and to climatic factors.

As late as 1968, there was not an English-language textbook on this subject and the only guide to it was the notes and informal presentations of Sanderson himself. These papers have been read by very few people, even specialists who should be interested, because by the time Sanderson got around to putting his thoughts down he had already begun his long slide into academic limbo. He had become somewhat bitter as a result, and his writing had become a bit too disrespectful and informal to be digested easily by the knowledge establishment.

How was it that someone with Sanderson's credentials managed to be labeled a crackpot? The answer is that, in years of training and more years of first-hand observation, Sanderson had come to the conclusion that much popular and expert knowledge, especially in the Western world, was often an inadequate and limited perception of reality, and sometimes pure myth.

One minor myth that inspired modest bouts of Sandersonian indignation was the popular myth of the Jungle. *Jungle* was originally a Persian word applied to low and scrubby growth, usually on hillsides, that impeded the passage of men and horses. The British took over the word and applied it, incorrectly, to the tall equatorial forests of the tropics. The thinking must have been that, since these forests were sufficiently different from their own, they warranted a foreign name.

There are true jungles all over the world—probably one of the densest is on the mountain slopes of the northwest coast of North America. But one place where jungles are conspicuously absent happens to be in the tall forests of great tropical rivers like the Amazon and the Congo. Nor is there much jungle in the forested regions of West Africa. For, in these forested places, the primary tree growth is so tall and so thickly foliaged that even sunlight has a difficult time penetrating. Under such conditions, then, there can be little small plant growth at ground level. The great trees form galleries, with their trunks as great columns, but at ground level passage is often quite easy. It is where this forest peters out in the uplands that one encounters jungle.

All of which has some relevance to our major theme. Let Sanderson speak!

> If one raises the subject of animal life in South America, everybody invariably yells "Green Hell," and thinks of the Amazon Basin. It is a funny thing, but there is nothing hellish about any "jungle" and rather especially about that of the Amazon. It is, like all equatorial forests, never too hot or too cold, singularly free of noxious insects, completely free from disease (provided you keep away from human beings and don't carry any pestilence in with you when you enter), is well supplied with food that is easy to obtain, has plenty of good water, and is not too badly infested with indigenous people who resent one's presence. There are poisonous snakes, and jaguars, but you really have to look for them.[1]

The popular conception is that "jungles" like the Amazon Basin are crawling with animal life, but in reality:

> ... its flora and fauna in no way compares with that of all the surrounding areas combined. In fact, it has manifestly been repopulated quite recently by streams of animals and plants from those areas.[2]

The reason for this seems to be that the Amazon Basin has only recently, in geological terms, been raised above the level of the sea. Even more recently, there have been inundations of various parts of it by the Atlantic. "Some Brazilian scientists claim that they have evidence that the last time this happened was only about the year 1200 B.C."[3]

If this is true, it not only explains adequately why the Amazon basin has relatively few different species of animals and plants; but it may also be significant for the pattern of civilized development in South America.

It has always been something of a mystery to archeologists why the earliest cultural developments in South America seem to have taken place on the eastern slopes of the Andes around the headwaters of the Amazon and its major northern tributaries, and the headwaters of the Orinoco. Why, of all places, near the source of the Rio Negro? Why not some place with a more forgiving environment, such as the areas where later high civilizations flourished.

Why on earth should cultural beginnings have been made in this "Green Hell"? To begin with, our popular misconceptions of the jungle probably contribute to this puzzlement. The forested region of the Rio Negro, Rio Uva and Rio Guaviare are not steaming and impassable at all, but fairly habitable under the tree canopy. Moreover, such an environment would be like home to some tropical forest people, assuming they came to the area and stimulated the otherwise puzzling cultural beginnings here.

But there is a second consideration. If parts of the Amazon basin were encroached upon by the Atlantic as recently as 1200 B.C., we are entitled to believe that the areas flooded would necessarily be the lowest. This means that the Amazon River and its major tributaries would likely be flooded by the ocean. The sea would extend inland many miles in a long, wide bay. The outlines of this tropical fjord can be plotted rather exactly for each few meters of assumed sea-rise. A very moderate rise in sea level would place the head of the prehistoric estuary precisely where cultural beginnings seem to have been made—that is, in Columbia where the Muisca culture first evolved.

We do not have to assume a worldwide rise in sea level to explain the Atlantic inundation of the Amazon area. The land could have risen and sunk alternately by several meters—or several hundred—with the same result. Such movement would accompany the rise of the Andes, a process that is not yet completed; tectonic activity associated with mountain-building

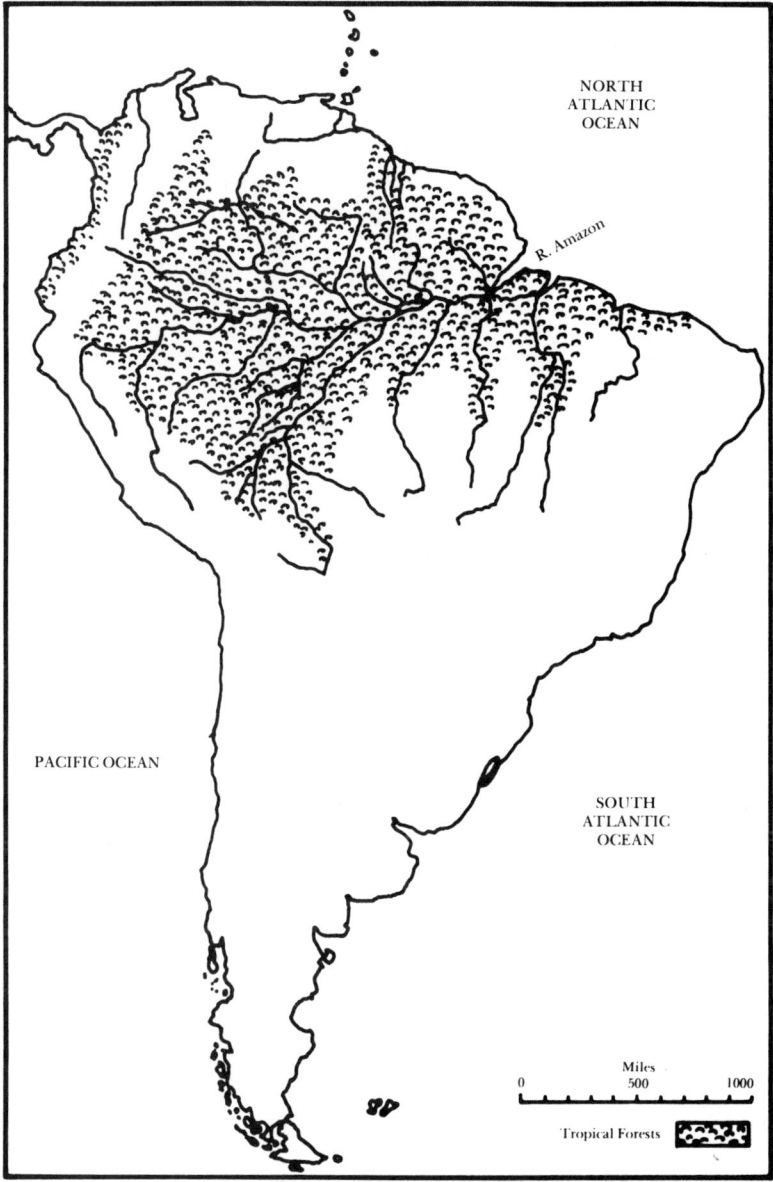

South America
Present Amazonian forested area (shaded) may have been inundated by the Atlantic in very recent times.

may well have temporarily raised or lowered the Amazon Basin several times within the memory of man. Such activity, in the form of major earthquakes, still alters the South American landscape, though not to the degree that would be necessary for a fairly recent flooding of a tract as vast as the Amazon Basin.

One thing is certain. In the midst of the Amazon Basin there are vast tracks of sand "islands" not too far inland from the rivers' edges. In many places, these sand dunes are so recent that they are not yet broken down into soil in which plants can take root. (A similar phenomenon occurs in more coastal regions of South America, where the line of sand islands parallels the present coast many miles inland. In Surinam, particularly, these sand dunes are a characteristic feature of the interior.[4])

These sandy strips in the midst of savannah or even forest seem to be ancient beaches where the sea surf once broke; yet they cannot be all that ancient because continental vegetation has not yet deposited more than the thinnest green veneer on most of them.

A glance at the map of South America will show that oceanic flooding of the Amazon watercourse would offer seafarers a natural path right to the eastern foothills. Yet such flooding would not materially increase the open ocean distance separating South America from West Africa. The Guiana Massif and the Caatinga uplands would have remained above water and would still have been the first land sighted by Atlantic seafarers. The major difference would have been that the Amazon would not have been even the huge river it is now, but a bay-estuary some 300 miles wide in places and about 1,500 miles long leading into the heart of South America.

Bearing in mind the possible geological profile of the Amazon about 1200 B.C., and the true nature of this jungle, American cultural beginnings in the eastern Andean uplands cease to be remarkable. It becomes natural and almost inevitable—assuming a West African contact.

Looking at a map alone one might logically ask: "Why would African visitors coming to South America not first land on the northeast point of Brazil, near Recife, and start culture there?" There are two answers. First, normal winds and currents would tend to sweep an African mariner to the north of the equator and would probably land a vessel quite close to the mouth of the Amazon, especially if the waterway were five or six times as large as it is today. Second, even if anyone did land on the northeast point of Brazil he certainly wouldn't stay there. The area is sparsely inhabited even today. This is the infamous "Caatinga," and it is appallingly dry. It would hold no allure for tropical voyagers, just as it holds small promise for modern colonists. Mariners would coast this arid land until led to the waterway of the Amazon. There, they would abruptly find different and a more hospitable world, and the waterway would beckon them to the interior of the continent.

If they penetrated to the head of this huge arm of the sea, visitors from Africa would find an environment very similar to that of West Africa in the neighborhood of Cape Verde. They would also have found people, probably American Indians similar to the people who inhabit the Amazon Basin today, who shared much their own lifestyle.

Did black African visitors come? Did they influence the rise of South American culture? It has to be said at once that the history of South America is even more mysterious than the history of pre-Columbian Mexico and Yucatan. In South America we don't have the confusion of the *tec*-nicalities, but we have absolutely no literary tradition to give even a distorted idea of what went on before the Incas came to power in the Andes.

> We have not even the beginnings of a written script to assist us in dating, as we have in Mesoamerica—unless we may consider as a sort of pictographic writing the great number of painted vases that have been preserved from certain periods and the figures woven into garments, fabrics and covers by the ancient weavers. But pictures of this kind are only an inadequate substitute for the hieroglyphs of the Maya and the pictographic signs of the Mexicans.[5]

Our notion of the pre-European history of South America, in its early phases, is entirely dependent upon archeological findings. This has some drawbacks:

> No doubt all these objects made of more impermanent materials . . . fell prey to the ravages of the humid subtropical climate, whereas the exceptionally dry climate on the Peruvian coast contributed in large measure to the preservation over the course of many centuries of such impermanent articles.[6]

Which is to say that more archeological work has been done in Peru than in any other place in South America simply

Museum für Volkerkünde, Berlin

because the Peruvian climate preserved more things for archeologists to study. Any historical reconstruction based upon archeology is therefore necessarily biased. We know very little about what went on in the eastern and forested part of the continent, although we do know that the earliest people in Peru seem to have come from there, since "very early strata of the Pacific coastal zone have yielded such typical elements of the jungle country as bark clothing and parrot-feather fans, as well as edible tropical plants such as manoic and ground nuts."[7]

Similarity of artistic motif—*coincidence or evidence of cultural contact? Figurines from Colombia (left) and West Africa. (Colombian figurine drawn after Disselhoff.)*

It seems that Peru was colonized by cultured people from "jungle country"; yet we know more about the Peruvians than about "jungle country" because the climate of the Pacific coast allowed the preservation of artifacts.

It is no exaggeration to say that we know almost nothing about the ancient cultures of the eastern Andean slopes, except that they must have existed prior to the beginnings of culture in Peru. We have two major areas of evidence: pottery and metalworking.

A certain style of pottery, incorporating the tradition of large urns, was first discovered on the island of Marajo in the Amazon delta. At first, this ceramic style was thought to be indigenous to the lower Amazon, but in 1956 the American archeologists Meggers and Evans found the same sort of pottery originating

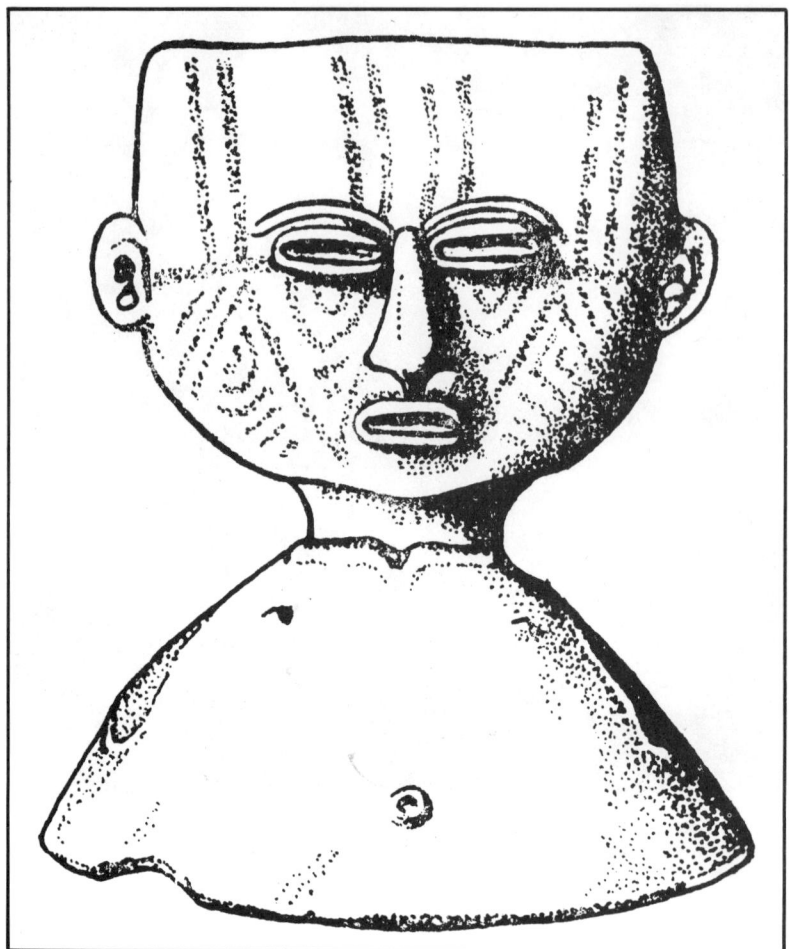
Museum für Volkerkünde, Berlin

from the upper reaches of the River Napo in eastern Ecuador, some 3,000 miles from the Amazon delta. Since then, several mid-Amazon sites have furnished proof that this pottery tradition spread from the eastern foothills down into the Basin. It did not reach the mouth of the Amazon until as late as about 1300 A.D., but there is no way to date the beginning of this style several thousand miles to the east.

With respect to the origin of metal-working in South America, we have only the vaguest notion:

> It is a fact—at least, according to the present state of our knowledge—that metal-working began in Peru at least five

Similarity of artistic motif—*coincidence or evidence of cultural contact? Colombian ceramic (left) and African mask. (Colombian figure drawn after Disselhoff.)*

hundred years earlier than in Mesoamerica. But we still do not know exactly where it originated, or the routes by which it spread from one part of America to another.[8]

All that can be said with certainty is that the first metal-working in America took on a peculiarly "African" profile. The early emphasis was upon the working of pure gold and pure copper. Only much later, in the Andes, was an alloy of gold and silver worked and some limited amounts of bronze produced. Even the earliest gold work shows a high degree of skill, as if the metal-working had been introduced by people with long experience in the art.

If the origins of South American metal-working are uncertain, there are some facts that are suggestive. In spite of the enormous quantities of gold extracted from the Incas by the

Spaniards, it appears that the "land of gold" lay to the east across the Andes. Accordingly, the Spanish sent several expeditions across the mountains and down into the foothills of Colombia near the borders of Venezuela and present-day Brazil. They were, of course, in search of El Dorado, of which they had heard tales told by Incas. This El Dorado was not originally a "city of gold" in the Spanish mind's eye, but was a person. El Dorado, the "gilded man," was, in fact, a mighty prince of a people so rich in gold that he himself was dusted completely with it. He was a prince of the Muisca culture in Colombia. It was the habit of El Dorado to dust himself with gold and then bathe it all off in a sacred lake on occasion, so rich were his people in this metal. The Spanish even found a tribe, called the Tairona, whose name means "goldsmiths."

It would seem at least likely, if not absolutely certain, that the tradition of South American metal-working originated where all traditions pointed to the "land of gold," which is to say probably in eastern Colombia, and perhaps also in eastern Ecuador and the neighboring areas of Venezuela. These ancient Colombians also worked pure copper, sometimes gilding it with the ubiquitous gold by a process using the acidic sap of a plant although no one understands exactly how this was accomplished.[9]

Even though great quantities of gold were appropriated by the Spanish, enough remained for archeologists to discover, and the Republican Bank of Colombia in Bogota now houses the richest collection of gold artifacts in the world.

The evidence of both pottery and metal-working points to the eastern Andean foothills as the origin of South American culture. Tributaries of the Amazon flow from both the north and the south, from regions as far apart as Colombia and Bolivia, including Ecuador, much of Brazil and even some of southern Venezuela. The cultural beginning may have been made almost anywhere in this vast tract of "Green Hell" and we may never discover the exact location. The existing distribution of languages, traditions and Indian tribes is probably of minimal assistance in trying to zero in on the cultural focal point because these people have been pushed around by the Incas, the Spanish and their own local foes for 3,000 years, and almost all languages, tribes and traditions have been displaced from their original homelands.

About the only thing that is clear is that culture came into

The Land of Gold

Peru from the north rather than from the south. This may provide an indication that the cultural center of ancient South America was in Colombia or Brazil rather than in Bolivia among the southerly Amazon tributaries. On the evidence, one is tempted to suggest that the Rio Negro and its tributaries, the Guaviare and the Uva, would be the most likely place to look. Unfortunately, if much of Amazonia was invaded by the Atlantic at the crucial period around 1200 B.C., we cannot expect to find significant ancient sites conveniently located along the

Greater Peru and Equador

river banks. Such sites will likely be in the "Green Hell" far from the present river courses.

If we cannot say precisely where this cultural epicenter came into being, are we on surer ground if we guess when it came into being? The first Peruvian metal-working dates from the Chavin culture about 500 B.C. We may be confident in assuming that metal-working in the "land of gold" began earlier and that it took some time for the tradition and knowledge of this new art to travel to the Pacific. How long? No one knows, of

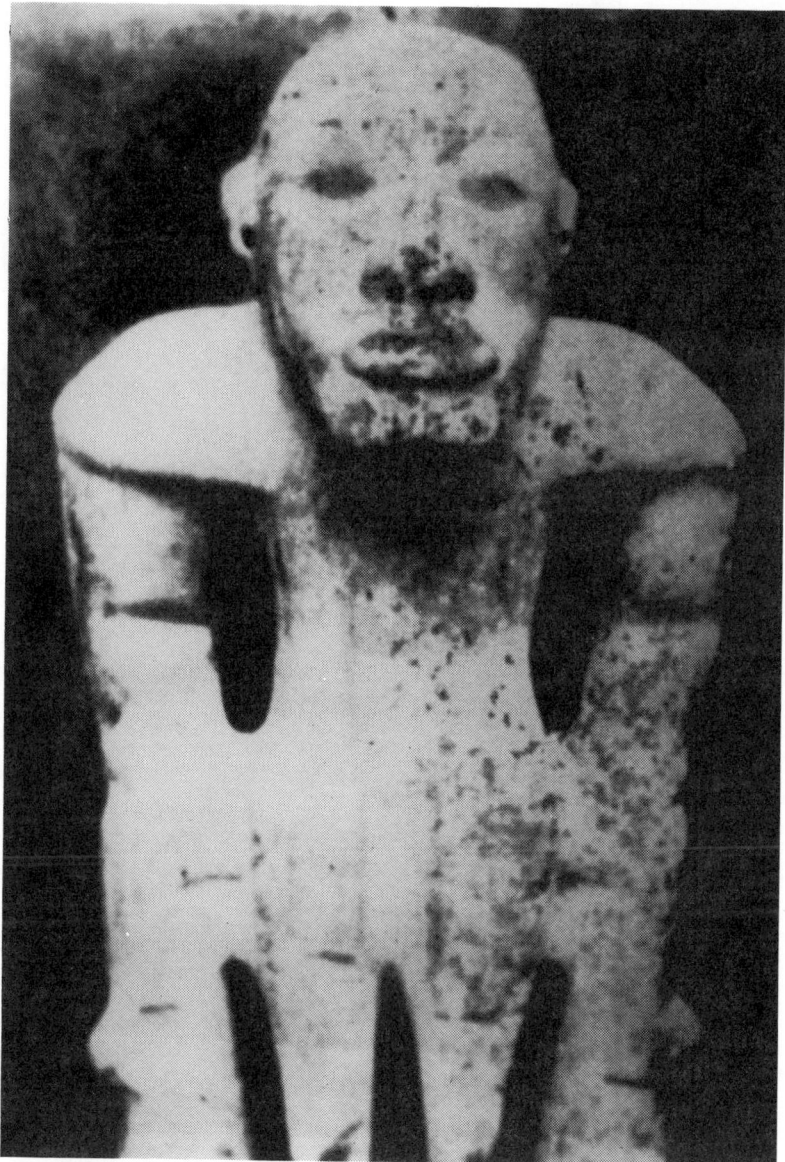

This Mexican figurine is suggestive of an anthropoid ape, *but there are no anthropoid apes in the Americas. The nearest representative of this primate group are the gorillas and chimpanzees of West Africa.*

course, but perhaps 500 years would be a reasonable estimate. If so, then metal-working began somewhere in upper Amazonia about the year 1000 B.C., give or take two or three centuries.

Aside from metal-working, these easterners eventually brought

Feather crown of Quetzalcoatl. *Did the American Indians learn feather work from tropical Africans? The art is unknown in the Mediterranean.*

to the Chavin of northern Peru the practice of mummification, the habit of stretching the ear-lobes with plug-like insertions, "jungle" food plants, and perhaps the art of weaving cotton.

Terms like Chavin culture and Chavin horizon take their names from the site of Chavin de Huántar in the Peruvian highlands, but the culture itself was widespread and there are Chavin sites on the upper reaches of the River Marañon and on the upper River Jequetepeque as well as on the coast in the valleys of the much smaller westward-flowing rivers draining into the Pacific. The distribution of the Chavin culture along these rivers suggest "highways" of cultural transmission from the eastern Andean slopes to the Pacific using river valleys to breach the mountain barrier.

Excavations carried out by Larco Hoyle at one Chavin site, the Chicama valley, revealed a number of rings carved of bone

These Peruvian bottle gourds *came originally from West Africa. Used for fishing net floats and water containers, bottle gourds were brought to the New World by man.*

which had at one time been worn on the fingers of some Chavin individual. The interesting thing about these rings is that lifelike little apes were modeled on each of them.[10] But there are no known "apes" in South America at all. These creatures are zoologically restricted to tropical Africa and Indonesia.

This, together with some of the culture-traits associated with Chavin, suggest African influence: ear-lobe plugs, mummification and gold-working. All reflect culture traits already existing in West Africa at this time.

Chavin was the first civilization, or proto-civilization, in Peru. These people built modest cities and temples. Somewhat later, immediately after Chavin, the Moche culture appeared in Peru. Moche (or Mochica) culture is characterized by a style of ceramics different from Chavin and by the first sign of pyramid-building. Mochica flourished about 750 A.D., but its origins go

Moche "house" model *once decorated the top of a clay vessel. But is this "house" not more likely to have been a temple or some other important building to have warranted a model of it? Disselhoff calls the rounded cone-like projections "roof combs." (Drawing after Disselhoff.)*

much further back and are probably contemporaneous with later stages of Chavin. The two cultures are obviously related, yet there appears to be some new infusion of ideas which produced Moche.

It is interesting to note that Moche pyramids are stepped pyramids made of mud-brick, not stone. In this, the early Moche pyramids resemble the earliest stepped pyramids of Meso-America that appeared about the same time. In both Chavin and Moche artistic motifs we find jaguar-man and bird-serpent symbolism very similar to Olmec and Mayan motifs. The bird-serpent conception is sufficiently similar to the Quetzalcoatl/Kukulcan of the Meso-Americans to cause Disselhoff and Linné to ask: "Is there some affinity here with the ancient Mexican rain god?"

I have discussed the jaguar-man motif and will discuss Quetzalcoatl and Kukulcan with specific reference to African zoology in Chapter Nine; but for now it seems sufficient to note the affinity between these Peruvian concepts and those of Meso-

African architecture features "roof combs"—*high, rounded cone projections on the roof line—similar to those on the "house" model from Moche horizons in Peru. The cones seem to be fewer, but more emphasized, in West Africa, and appear mostly on temples or other important buildings, such as fortresses. They may originally have been "horns" of the sun-as-ram belief complex. The mosque at Djenne on the Niger is an excellent example of this style.*

America. This suggests some common origin in the headwaters of Amazonia.

Of particular significance, possibly, is a small Moche figurine—actually a fragment from a ceramic vessel—which depicts a Moche house. The roof-line of this house bears a decoration of tall, rounded cones. The house is rather obviously molded of clay. These "roof combs" (an inadequate and inaccurate description) are strikingly reminiscent of West African architecture.

We are certainly not justified in attributing all culture elements of Chavin, Moche and the earlier Muisca in Colombia to black African influence. If African visitors came, as seems likely, they contributed to existing cultural ideas in a fusion. It seems to me that the emphasis upon gold-work, the ear-lengthening, the jaguar-man and the bird-serpent conceptions, the mud-brick pyramids and the house architecture betray some African characteristics. (Chavin and Moche ceramic traditions may do so as well, for one particular characteristic idea in American pottery suggests African cultural input. See Chapter Nine.)

I suggest that an early fusion of black African and native Amerindian cultures produced something new and vital and that this vitality began an advanced cultural epoch in the

Clay house at Kano, Nigeria

Americas. In addition, aside from the culture-traits listed above, it is very likely that black Africans introduced the plantain and the bottle gourd at this time, and may have taught the Americans how to utilize their native cotton. (See Chapter Eight.)

Although we know nothing for certain about the day-to-day customs of Chavin and Moche folk, some later Inca behavior may well trace back to these early founding cultures. The sun-worship of the Incas seems to reflect the ritual gold-dust-washing baths of El Dorado. In fact, the legend of how the first Inca came to power is very similar to El Dorado's antics. Sinchi Rocha, the first historic ruler of the Inca dynasty, clad himself in burnished gold and appeared at the mouth of a cavern above Cuzco just as the rays of the morning sun fell upon him. The local population was dazzled by this apparition and apparently believed Sinchi Rocha when he maintained that he'd come from the sun to govern them.

El Dorado's bath seems to be a similar, but much more ancient, ritual, since Sinchi Rocha dates from 1100 to about

1140 A.D. It may well be that Sinchi Rocha did not bemuse the locals at all; perhaps for reasons unknown, he went through an ancient and agreed-upon ceremony of assuming a sun-kingship, possibly as a war-leader in some great common threat to local tribes. Sinchi means "war chief."

The sun-kingship obviously predates Sinchi Rocha and the later Incas, although the Incas evolved the idea much further than anyone else, in order to meld the interests of a great confederation of peoples into an empire. Sun-worship probably dates from long before Chavin times—certainly the Chavin temples are oriented east-west—but the sun/gold/El Dorado type politics of eastern Colombia were probably of Chavin origin, adopted by the Incas at a later date. There was also a sun-kingship in West Africa.

One other aspect of Inca kingship may hint at ancient origins and African ones. In spite of the sun-kingship, the Incas, like the Egyptians, often indulged in brother-sister marriages. This practice is generally indicative of a matrilinear society, or at least matrilinear succession of the kingship. It was a system in use not only in Egypt but also in parts of West Africa.

Then, the Incas took the modest Chavin and Moche ear-plugs and emphasized ear-lengthening into a token of nobility.

Civilization did not develop in Peru along exactly the same lines as in Meso-America. This is a function of Peruvian geography. Most of coastal Peru is a desert. Small rivers flow down from the mountains to the Pacific; it is only in these river valleys that a sizable population can be sustained, with the assistance of irrigation.

Cultures developed in these valleys, but the desert between valleys prevented any great degree of fusion among them until Inca times. In fact, the consolidation of various differing cultures and people into one "empire" was the greatest Inca achievement. In the general imagination, the Incas are supposed to be the ancient rulers of Peru, but in reality they are not very ancient at all. Only 500 years before Columbus, the Incas were a tribe no more or less obscure than many others in the Peruvian highlands, sharing the common legacy of earlier Chavin and Moche (and Nazca, Tiahuanaco and Chimu) evolution. But somehow, and for some unexplainable reason, the Incas managed to weld the separated coast cultures into one administrative unit.

Much that we call Inca probably existed as the common fund of custom and belief among many coastal societies. The Inca empire was a federation of customs and culture more than the imposition of the dominant culture of the conquering people. There were traditionally only twelve Incas who ruled in succession. The first was Manco Capac, although Sinchi Rocha became the first real ruler of a sizable polity, and the last was Atahualpa, who was murdered by the Spanish. Incas ruled from about 1100 to 1533. In those brief 400-odd years all the great wonders of Inca rule were created: marvelous roads and walls crossing awesome mountain obstacles; cities of stone perched on Andean peaks; suspension bridges spanning entire valleys.

But the greatest wonder must be Inca society itself. Philip Ainsworth Means has written about the death of Atahualpa:

> With him died not only the Inca Empire but also an entire and unique politico-social philosophy and a civilization based upon the happiness of all. Money, lust and gold hunger entered Peru along with Christianity.[11]

It was a society in which rich and poor had access to justice on a basis so equal that we of the West have not yet rivaled it, in which the necessity for work was balanced with guaranteed security of individuals, in which there seemed to be an almost conscious effort to refuse to adopt technology that would inevitably undermine the psychology and economy of the people. It was a sort of "capital-communism": it incorporated the best aspects of both of the ideologies that presently compete for our world, and seems to have avoided the impracticalities, inhumanities and intolerance of each. It was, in fact, a social balance we of the West have never been able to achieve and may well be psychologically incapable of conceiving, but which we might do much worse than to emulate.

For this reason alone, the influence of white gods from Europe must be re-evaluated. There seems to be no doubt that white people did come to Peru and to Meso-America. In Meso-America they may very well have had an unhappy and inhumane influence, but in Peru—if they came and even if they ruled—their numbers and cultural impact cannot have been great because Peruvian society bears not the remotest resemblance to any culture yet constructed by white men. However, in its emphasis on fusion and accommodation of peoples, beliefs and customs, Peruvian society as it flourished under the Incas does very much resemble the African way of expansion as analyzed by people like Davidson and Herskovits.

It is now time to investigate whether black Africans of approximately 1000 B.C. could have expanded across the Atlantic to bring their material offerings and their tradition of fusion to the New World.

6

The Matter of Boats

Atlantic crossings have been made by almost every likely floating contrivance, and by many that were less than likely: row boat; rubber raft; kayak; *Tinkerbelle*, a thirteen-foot sailing dinghy; and even by a World War II surplus amphibious jeep appropriately named *Half Safe*. Transatlantic voyages have also been made by copies of various ancient boats: replica Viking ships; Severin's leather boat, constructed according to medieval Irish specifications; and Heyerdahl's *Ra II*, a boat of reeds held together with rope made by Bolivian Indians, but similar to ancient reed boats depicted by Egyptian models and mural representations.

In the trade wind zone, at least, the Atlantic can be crossed by just about everything. It is probably only a matter of time before some adventurer manages it in a bathtub. In fact, the wonder seems to be that the seaward shores of the Barbados are not littered with floating rubbish from Africa, since the currents and trade winds carry anything floatable from Africa to the New World.

The trick, of course, is to stay on that floating object through the occasional gale and to remain alive throughout the crossing. Dr. Bombard set off across the Atlantic in a small life-raft without either food or water and reached the other side alive. He caught fish and plankton for food and used fish juice for water, but grew to detest the "insipid fish juice." Taking food and water for thirty to sixty days would certainly make the trip a great deal more pleasant.

Although there are gales and hurricanes in season along the trade wind route from Africa to America, most voyagers in these latitudes speak of gentle crossings, warm day following warm day and a more or less constant fair wind. Occasionally, the trade winds do not dip as far south as expected and crossings by sail are slowed. In 1951, when Dr. Bombard boarded his raft,

Portuguese painting of sailing canoes on the Congo estuary

and Anne Davidson set sail in her twenty-foot sloop *Felicity Anne*, the trade winds were fickle and both voyages were longer than average. But, generally, some form of sailing boat will average about one hundred miles per day, while something like a raft or a reed boat will average about sixty miles a day.[1]

It is absurd to have to prove the ability of black Africans to cross the Atlantic to the New World. They developed four different types of vessels. Their dugout canoes were up to eighty feet in length with a carrying capacity of more than ten tons. Early Portuguese accounts relate that these dugouts were accustomed to make trading voyages of 100 leagues along the coast. They also used a reed raft or boat similar to Heyerdahl's *Ra II*, which not only crossed to America, but set out from Morocco rather than Cape Verde, so Heyerdahl sailed much farther than a West African would have to in order to reach the same landfall. It is also likely that West Africans modified dugouts to increase the freeboard by adding planks sewn together and placed on edge along the natural gunwale. It is barely possible, also, that

African dugouts lashed together

the West Africans may have sewn planked vessels to create craft with a wider beam than was possible by hollowing out even the largest jungle logs. And they had log rafts.

It is also known that the West Africans would occasionally lash two dugout canoes together, side-by-side, catamaran fashion. These black African canoes resembled Polynesian double canoes, and no one doubts the sailing ability of those.

But even a single canoe would be capable of crossing from Cape Verde to Brazil. (Canadian Captain J. C. Voss even circumnavigated the earth in an average-sized Northwest Coast Haida dugout canoe, although it must be admitted that Voss' craft was schooner rigged.)

It appears that some West African dugout canoes resembled the lines of ancient Egyptian sea-going boats with stem and stern upswept out of the water. Their sails, too, look faintly Egyptian.

Large canoe being paddled

(Someone like Emperor Kankan Musa of Mali, a medieval Islamic monarch, would probably have possessed the pan-Arabic dhow with its lateen sailing rig. This type of sail allowed a ship to navigate to windward and, in fact, da Gama's ship incorporated this rig which the Portuguese borrowed from the Moorish world. According to Alan Villiers, who sailed aboard a dhow, the lateen sail "pulls like a mule," but is an inconvenient rig for use in beating against highly variable winds because the boom, which is long and cumbersome, must be shifted to the lee side of the mast with every change of tack if maximum efficiency is to be extracted. In a region of prevailing winds coming from a reliable direction, such as with the Indian Ocean monsoons, lateen-rigged dhows have carried cargo for ages. Such a ship would be no less suited for a trade wind passage from Africa to America and there is little doubt that the ships of Mali, circa 1250-1350 A.D., in the days of Kankan Musa and his predecessor, would have been dhows.)

In the period before Christ, it is likely that black Africans from the neighborhood of Cape Verde would have used dugout canoes primarily. The term *canoe* is somewhat misleading for

Large canoe with mast on the Niger

these African boats. Westerners know that a dugout canoe is limited by the size of tree from which it is made; but, as they have their own trees in mind, their mental picture of a dugout canoe is of something very narrow and not very long. However, the tropical equatorial forests of West Africa produce trees of monumental proportions. Dugouts made from these trees were often longer than medieval European ships.

In the 1500s, Pacheco Pereira wrote: "In this country are to be found the largest canoes, made of a single trunk, that are known in the whole Ethiopia of Guinea; some are so large that they hold 80 men. They travel distances of 100 leagues [300 miles]."[2] One hundred years later, Pieter de Marees saw one "cut out of a tree which was five and thirty foot long and five foot broad and three foot high, which was as big as a shallop."[3]

The longest West African dugout canoes would probably be about eighty feet in length and ten feet in beam with a height from "keel" to gunwale of five to six feet. Such a canoe would be the same size as the largest Viking "long ships," and twice the size of Severin's traditional Irish leather boat in which he crossed the North Atlantic.

A canoe "as big as a shallop" would be much larger, for instance, than Davidson's *Felicity Anne* and comparable in size to the famous "Virtue" class of five-ton wooden yachts which have numerous transatlantic voyages as well as one circumnavigation of the earth to their credit.

The important point is that the canoes would have been much stronger than modern wooden yachts. The strength of a wooden boat is in its fastenings, which hold the planks to the ribs and the ribs to the keel. A dugout has no fastenings as it is one piece of wood. It is therefore inherently stronger than a modern wooden yacht of the same plank thickness and incomparably stronger than a Viking long ship of similar size. Yet, Western historians take pride in the naval architecture of the medieval North Europeans, consider Viking boats to be the ancestors of "real" ships, and denigrate canoes of comparable size and much greater strength. While we accept the voyages of the Norse as historical fact, we smile at the thought of people undertaking passage to America in giant canoes—even though these canoes were superior in every basic respect to any vessel possessed by Lief Ericsson.

It is not so much a question of whether black Africans could have crossed the Atlantic from the area of Cape Verde to the

New World, because an average-size canoe with reasonable luck could hardly not complete such a voyage once caught in the currents and trade winds. Some twenty-five to forty days after leaving Cape Verde it would be cast up on the shores of South America somewhere between the mouth of the Amazon and Trinidad. To be caught in the America-bound currents, such a canoe would have to venture only about fifty to one hundred miles offshore. This, we know, was more than possible. (Pereira records that the Africans traveled "100 leagues" in their dugouts, while de Marees assures us that the Africans used their craft "to fish or go to sea withal.")

The real question is whether, once having arrived in the New World, any of these Africans could have returned, against the winds and currents, in order to bring news of their discovery back home. We know that black Africans reached the New World at an early date because of artistic representations. But could some have returned to Africa? A few must have made the west-to-east passage. Otherwise what would be the basis for the Kankan Musa's predecessor's belief that there were limits to the neighboring sea and that another shore might be found to the west where he sent his ships? Columbus' certainty of land west of Cape Verde also suggests strongly that black Africans of the region had been told by returning mariners that lands lay beyond the sunset.

How could Africans of about 1000 B.C. have managed the return voyage across the Atlantic? It is barely possible for a canoe crew to paddle across the Atlantic in the doldrums south of the trade-wind zone right at the equator. In the doldrums, as the name implies, there is no prevailing wind, so sailing ships were often becalmed for weeks in this region. But the doldrums are lively with minor squalls and rainstorms, and there is a great deal of oceanic life in this area. Therefore, a doldrum passage by paddle in a good-sized canoe is very possible, especially by people accustomed to living on fish. Fresh water would not be in short supply because there are showers in the doldrums continuously. The distance from the coast of Brazil to the coast of Africa by this route would be about 2,000 miles. There are some currents in this confused area between great westward-tending flows of air and water, and some of the currents run eastward. But all are weaker than those to the north or south.

Navigation would present few problems. All the mariners

would have to do is paddle continuously in the direction of the rising sun, just as they had followed the setting sun to the New World. Their journey would take about 100 days or perhaps slightly less, for at about 15 degrees west longitude the canoe would encounter north-flowing currents that follow the contour of the African coast around the Gulf of Guinea. These would not only speed the paddlers' eastward progress, but would deposit them very near to Cape Verde. If the voyage began from the mouth of the Amazon, there would be some slingshot effect, as the river's flow extends 100 miles into the sea.

Nonetheless, it would be a long and tiring passage. Yet, it would be a considerably safer passage, and a much shorter one, than that experienced by the several modern adventurers who have rowed across the Atlantic in higher latitudes. (Chay Blyth and John Ridgway traveled almost twice as far as the distance separating Brazil and Cape Verde in *English Rose III*.) So the notion of black Africans paddling back across the Atlantic is not far-fetched. It could not have happened many times, but only one such adventure would be needed to establish among the blacks of Cape Verde the knowledge of land beyond the western horizon.

However, it is also possible that passages may have been made against wind and current by sail. In order to do this, the black Africans of 1000 B.C. would have had to know the principle of the lee-board, to prevent or alleviate leeway. They would also have had to understand the principle of using a sail to beat into the wind; that is, they would have had to have learned that the edge of a sail, if stiff enough, can be set into the wind and the boat, if equipped with leeboards, can make good a course of between 90 degrees and 45 degrees against the wind.

Assuming that they knew these two principles, West Africans could set a passage against the trade winds for part of the distance, through the doldrums for another part, and into the fair or following winds off the African coast. Such a voyage would take, possibly, sixty days from the area of Natal in Brazil to Cape Verde, but it might take as little as thirty days.

Modern Western historians, and especially historians concerned with naval architecture, are very chary about acknowledging the sailing abilities of some "primitive" people and are doubly so when it comes to granting any sort of ability to sail to windward. I think, therefore, that some perspective needs to be established. Until about 1450, Europeans possessed rather poor ocean-going ships compared with those of both ancient and contemporary peoples. European ship construction possessed only one inherent virtue: it produced wooden ships in large sizes. But this virtue was discovered only about 1500 and was not a method of construction they adopted because they knew it was or would become superior. The Europeans developed their style of ship construction out of necessity.

There were large European dugouts in ancient times and some examples are preserved from Holland and from Italy. Doubtless, whenever the opportunity arose, Europeans made and preferred large dugouts to boats. But the opportunity cannot have occurred too often. The deciduous trees of Europe may have great diameter, but they seldom boast a trunk straight enough for a dugout of any length. The tall, straight evergreens of Europe are pygmies compared to those of the tropics or the Northwest Coast of America. Nor did the Europeans possess suitable reeds except along the Mediterranean coast or straight, light and strong trees comparable to the balsa of South America.

If the Europeans were to develop true seaworthy boats of any size, they were forced to build vessels from smaller pieces. The keel was simply the longest and straightest piece of timber that could be found that was of adequate size; the frames were smaller pieces of adequate size, which were bent to the proper shape by soaking and steaming. Alternatively, naturally curved sections that fitted the curve of the hull form made a virtue of necessity. Planking, too, was a necessity, if one was going to make ships larger than the available timber; these small planks were fixed to other pieces of the framework to make a hull. A ship with a keel and frame was the only boat Europeans could make, given their natural materials. Yet, we are so used to thinking of this as a "normal" boat, we forget that it is merely a practical solution to the problem of limited resources.

The variable weather of European latitudes, including that strange phenomenon called winter, resulted in sailing conditions that were frequently stormy and often cold. It therefore became necessary that a water craft offer protection for both crew and cargo.

Since the North Europeans, at least as of early Viking times, had neglected to invent the saw (something that the Egyptians had managed to contrive by 2700 B.C.), they were unable to cut planks accurately enough that they could be laid on the hull edge-to-edge in what is known as "carvel fashion"; instead,

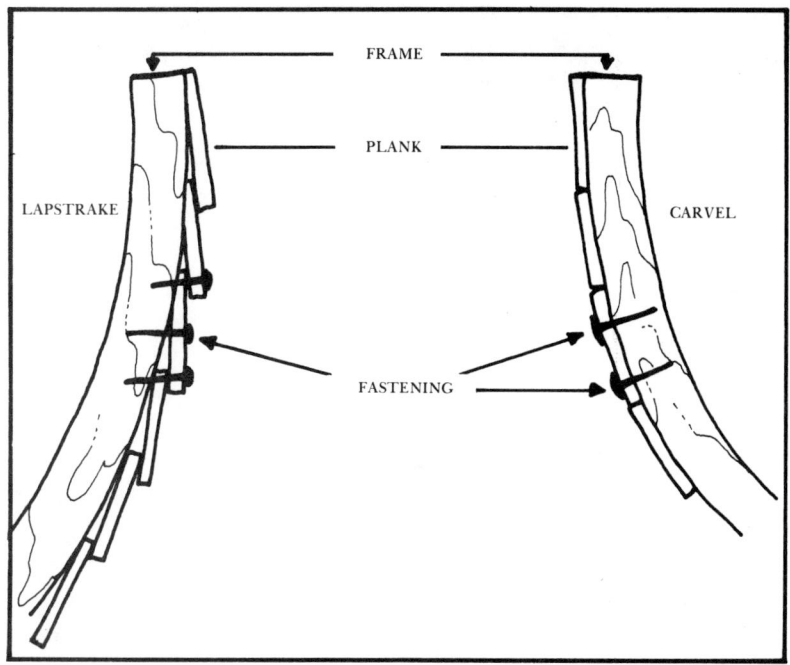

Planking Methods

Because Northern Europeans had not invented the saw by early Medieval times, they could not cut planks accurately enough to lay them edge to edge in the carvel method of construction. Nonetheless, using their limited material resources, they produced seaworthy boats like this beautiful Viking ship (see next page).

again making a virtue of necessity, they overlapped the upper planks over the lower in what is called "lapstrake" construction. Obviously, planks overlapped in this fashion cannot be as securely fastened to the frames as planks fastened flush against the frame. The bottom part of the plank will be separated from the frame surface by the width of the plank below. But even this, in the hindsight of Western historians of naval architecture, has been hailed as a virtue. As they see it, the Viking ships were seaworthy because they "gave" in a seaway. That they often "gave" in a way that alarmed their crews and sometimes "gave way" altogether with the loss of ship and crew has not lessened the experts' admiration for these vessels.

I am not trying to denigrate European ships and shipbuilding. On the contrary, I stand in great admiration of it. The wonder is that a people so ill-equipped with natural material

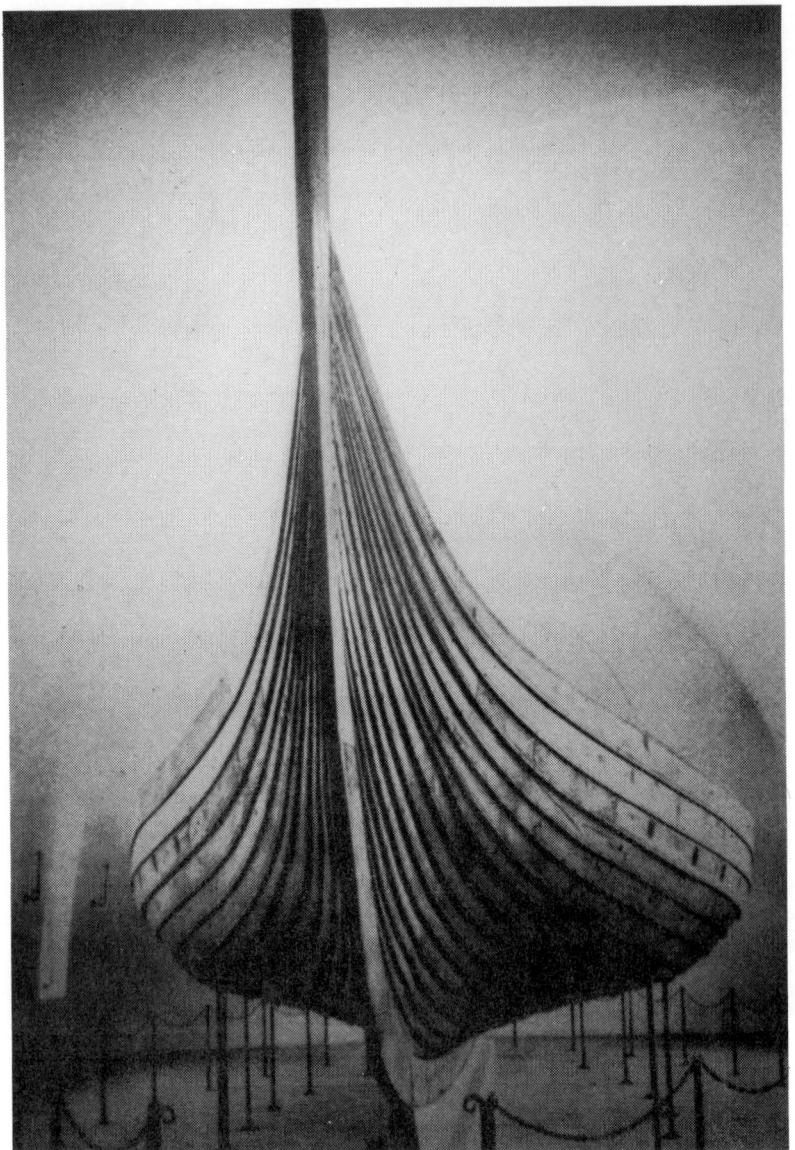

The Gokstad Ship

could still have contrived such seaworthy vessels. But the path of our development should not compel our scholars and our sailors to ridicule the oceanic achievements of other peoples who, blessed with more adequate building materials, could have produced seaworthy vessels and skills without following the complicated, laborious methods that seem proper to us.

The question remains: could black Africans of 1000 B.C. sail to windward so that a west-to-east crossing of the Atlantic from Brazil to Cape Verde could be accomplished? My own opinion is that any people who possessed sails of a certain type and configuration, and paddles of a certain configuration, possessed the means to sail to windward. Both the black Africans and the earliest Egyptians had the requisite type of sail and paddle to accomplish this feat. If this ability is not stressed in their maritime accounts, it may be that it simply was not very important to them and that they did not use this ability except in unusual circumstances. The desire to return home against wind and current from the New World across a couple of thousand miles of ocean would certainly rank as an unusual circumstance.

The evidence suggests, but does not prove, that black Africans of the Cape Verde area, no less than the partly black Egyptians themselves, knew how to sail into the wind, even if their normal commerce made the technique too cumbersome for ordinary use. Much of the evidence involves basic navigational principles that many readers may not be familiar with.

Most people may look at a sail being swelled by the wind and conclude that it is obvious that a sail "pushes" a boat through the water. Obvious, but untrue. A sail, even if filled by wind coming from directly behind a boat, does not push. It pulls a boat through the water. The reason for this is that a sail either stops the wind, or distorts the air flow, so that a vacuum is formed in front of the sail. It is this vacuum and the resulting difference in air pressure that pulls a sail in the direction of the vacuum.

With this in mind, it becomes clear how a boat can sail into the wind. No boat can sail directly against the wind, of course, but a properly equipped boat can sail at any angle of up to 45 degrees into the wind. Progress directly against the direction of wind is made by a series of zig-zags of up to 45 degrees in the direction from which the wind is blowing. Each zig or zag at an angle to the wind is called a tack.

Knowing that a sail pulls by creating a vacuum in front of itself and the boat, it is easy to understand how a boat can be pulled through the water into the wind. There are two sets of requirements that allow this to happen: one for the sail and one for the boat itself.

First, the sail must have an edge of some stiffness so as to cut the wind and so that the entire sail does not simply bag and

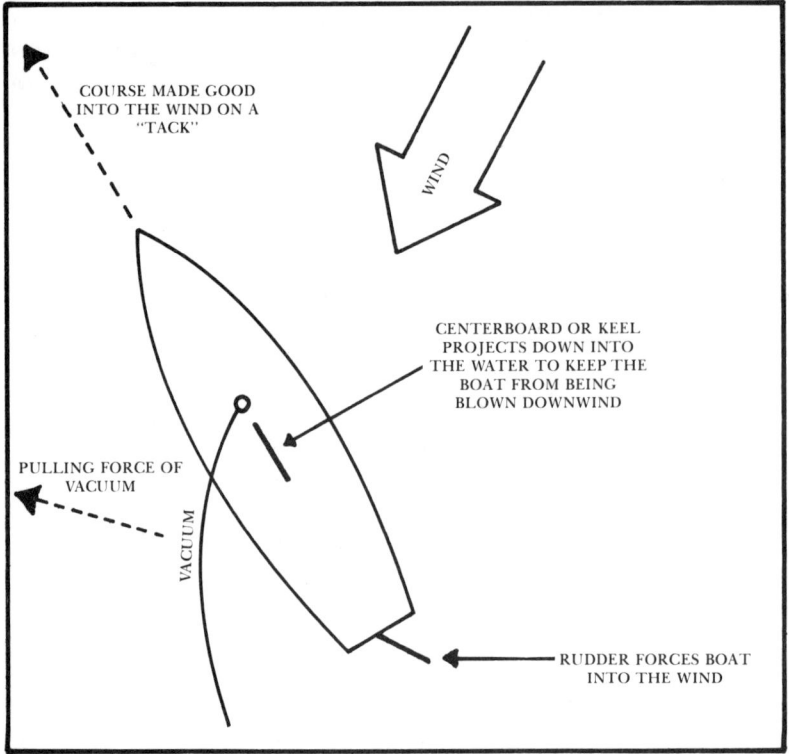

Sailing into the Wind
A resolution of all the conflicting forces produces a course of about 45° into the wind. In spite of the centerboard, the boat will be blown somewhat downwind on every tack. A course directly into the wind consists of a series of these zig-zag tacks. Commercial sailing vessels avoided sailing against prevailing winds as much as possible.

collapse in the wind. This edge may be created by sewing rope onto the edge of the cloth and drawing it taut, or by attaching the leading edge of the sail directly to something stiff like a mast or boom. The sail must also curve, or otherwise distort the wind as it passes over the sail, so that a vacuum is formed on the front of the sail.

The curve of the sail and the required stiffness of the leading edge may also be created by using a sail material other than limp cloth. A sail of woven reeds, for example, may possess an edge stiff enough to use without a rope, mast or boom attached to it. This is the solution arrived at by the Chinese, possibly by some types of early Egyptian-African vessels and by some Polynesian craft. Rock drawings from Nubia from the predynastic period show sails of mat, probably woven papyrus or palm leaf, supported on a single mast.

Now for the second set of requirements—that of the boat itself. Something must project down into the water to prevent the boat from being blown too much in the direction of the wind. All boats sailing into the wind will be blown somewhat downwind (this is called "leeway"), but the goal is to reduce this to a minimum. Almost any flat area projected into the water can act against the boat being blown "sideways." Some peoples, like the Incas, have used *guara* boards stuck between logs of a raft; others used paddles stuck vertically down over the side, which served just as well. These are exactly like the "leeboards" used on some smaller sailing dinghies and even on large Dutch yachts. (In fact, the first "yachts" and the principle of the leeboard were introduced to Europe by the Dutch about 1600 after they had come in contact with Indonesian vessels that could sail into the wind.) The deep keel or centerboard on modern boats works on the same principle.

Records show that Europeans were rather recently introduced to the art of windward sailing; the Incas, the Chinese and the Indonesians had all learned the principle of lateral resistance much earlier. The Chinese evolved a particularly unique and effective answer: they lowered the rudder itself far into the water so that this single structure acted as both a rudder and a centerboard.

Experience has shown that anything, be it centerboard, keel, or whatever, stuck down into the water is most effective if it is long and relatively narrow. Of course, it must also be as thin as possible to cut the water and reduce as much as possible the resistance to forward motion. Contemporary engineers would say that the keel, centerboard or leeboard should have a "high aspect ratio." The ancient Inca *guara* boards show that these Amerindians knew this long before we did. A typical *guara* will project about five feet down into the water, but be only 5 to 10 inches wide, and as thin as possible.

I believe that the ancient Egyptians and black Africans were familiar with the principles of windward sailing because of the distinctive shape of their paddles. The blades were shaped like a greatly elongated heart and came to a point at the bottom. Anyone who has ever had instruction in paddling a canoe knows that it is important not to take too deep a stroke, that a shallow stroke serves as well. The paddles common to Egyptian and black African peoples are too long and too narrow for truly effective paddling, but they do have a high aspect ratio. I believe their shape was a compromise so they could serve two different functions: paddling and use as leeboards.

I believe that from the earliest times, these paddles could be lashed vertically down from the gunwhales of reed boats or on dugouts, to be used as leeboards. (Heyerdahl aboard *Ra I* and *II* used his Egyptian-style paddles in this way when his steering oars broke, and was able to sail across the wind, at least, using these paddles *guara*-fashion.)

The Africans from earliest recorded times had sails with an "edge" and paddles that could be used as leeboards. I think it is rather likely, therefore, that they were capable of sailing to windward.

I do not mean to suggest that they could sail to windward well, but only that they could do so to some limited extent. It is beyond doubt that such ships as those in Nubian rock drawings could sail across the wind—that is to say, at 90 degrees to it. Probably they could sail "into" the wind in a limited fashion, say, within 60 to 70 degrees of the wind direction.

This ability would have been of little use in all but the broadest rivers, as it would be difficult not to run aground on one side or the other with each zig or zag. Then, too, the sail must be retrimmed for each tack, and this took a great deal of effort. It would have been easier to paddle. On the Nile this is particularly true because, although the Nile flows north, the prevailing wind blows toward the south. One could simply drift downstream, and sail upstream with a following wind and simple sails.

It is on the ocean that windward sailing would come into its own, but still in a more limited fashion than one might think. Its main use would be for maneuvering into and out of harbors. But, even if the sailors were willing to retrim the complicated sails and rigging with each tack, there is another consideration. Sails and rigging suitable for windward work are not the most efficient for use with a following wind. Commercial vessels in the ancient world might well have spurned the use of windward rigs because, with plenty of time and no rush, it was easier and more efficient to plan voyages and rigs for downwind sailing.

Windward ability of boats and windward sailing has only been stressed in the last few decades with the advent of sport sailing. The greatest (but erroneous) sensation of speed is to be had from "beating to windward," and in tests of skill windward work becomes important. But it has never been so in commercial craft for long-distance voyages. Although the principle of sailing to windward had long been known in Europe, and even though sport boats, coastal trading vessels and pilot boats of the mid-1800s had a great deal of windward ability, the great clippers were solely downwind ships; and voyages were planned to take advantage of fair prevailing winds and currents even if the course strayed far from the shortest straight line port-to-port.

Some clippers could not go to windward at all or even sail efficiently across the wind. One clipper, bound from Sydney to Perth in Australia against the prevailing winds and currents, tried unsuccessfully for a week to beat through the Bass Straits. Then the captain gave up, warped his ship and circumnavigated the world, reaching Perth by way of Cape Horn! Anyone judging our knowledge from clippers alone would conclude that Europeans of 1840 had not learned how to sail to windward. Only an examination of rather minor shipping would reveal this ability.

Our records of early shipping are scanty, the first artistic representations being drawings of river craft from the upper reaches of the Nile and these would not necessarily reveal anything about the little used ability to sail to windward. Until about 1200 B.C. our knowledge of ships comes mainly from Egyptian artwork; these records concern mainly important people and, therefore, important ships. We see the best ocean trading ships of rulers like Hatshepsut, which are likely to have been "square-riggers" like clippers, or we see river barges and boats used by princes and pharoahs. Other than this "monumental" shipping, we see representations of papyrus rafts used mainly by noblemen as platforms for duck and hippo hunting, in marshes, where boats would logically be poled or paddled rather than sailed.

Evidence of vessels used for windward sailing or rigged "fore and aft"—would naturally come from drawings of small, coastal vessels in minor maritime commerce. Such evidence is so rare, even in later ancient history, that:

> Until a few decades ago there was near unanimity of
> opinion: the ancients, it was claimed, used no sail other

than the square sail. As we can now tell from representations that have come to light in the last half-century, they knew at least three types of fore-and-aft rig. The best attested is the sprit, which was in use from, at the latest, the second century B.C.[4]

Although the sail shape shown in the Nubian drawings is square, the sails are undoubtedly made of mat, as the cross-hatching indicates the weaving of wide strips. They resemble the square-shaped sails of North Chinese junks which, whatever their shape, functioned as fore-and-aft sails for windward work. It is the stiffness of a mat sail that creates an "edge" that allows it to work into the wind.

There is one further piece of supporting evidence. The sails depicted in the Nubian rock drawings are small compared to the size of hull. If the craft was designed solely for downwind sailing, a much larger sail would be called for. But if, a long narrow craft, like a dugout or long planked boat, was intended to sail across the wind or against it, a very small sail would be essential. The stability of such a vessel would not be great and the wind pressure of tacking with a large sail would tend to capsize a long, narrow and shallow hull. A small sail is demanded and that is what we see in the drawings.

But if windward sailing was not much use on a river, why should we see representations of sailing ships of possible windward ability on the upper Nile? The answer to this is very possibly that in 3000 B.C. the Nile was much broader than it is now. Parts of it, even in Nubia, may have been large lake-like swellings of the stream. Such lakes still exist today in Ethiopia, near the source of the Nile.

> Around the middle of the Neolithic period, about 5000 B.C., rain became common also in Egypt, and this favorable climate persisted well into the country's historical period, to the beginning of the Sixth Dynasty. The surrounding desert once more became steppe, with elephants, antelopes, rhinoceroses and giraffes. Along the Nile were great marshes where papyrus grew.[5]

We may imagine that there were also great lakes at points where the Nile valley widened out, although, to my knowledge, no one has mapped the probable outlines of these ancient lakes.

Boats with some windward sailing ability probably developed on such lakes, where they would be most useful, and I believe that it is these that are shown in the rock drawings.

At any rate, a "Heyerdahl"-type voyage from Africa to the New World is unnecessary to "prove" that black Africans reached western lands. There is little doubt that a typical West African dugout of large proportions could make the journey. What might be interesting and worthwhile to attempt is the opposite crossing, to determine whether black Africans could have returned to bring tidings of their discovery to the Old World. Blyth and Ridgway have proved that men can row across the Atlantic, and so did doryman Blackburn before them, so there is not much doubt that a stout crew of paddlers could cross a much narrower stretch of water in a better climatic zone. But could a dugout, or a three-plank vessel, rigged as shown on the rock drawings and using lashed paddles for leeboards, make the west-to-east Atlantic crossing? Could such a craft even sail to windward?

To my knowledge, the only ancient evidence of dugout-type craft with sails occurs on these Nubian rock drawings of circa 3000 B.C. I have not been able to find any reliable account of a West African craft powered by anything other than paddles in early European times (except, of course, for the reference to Kankan Musa's medieval ships). However, it is known that people migrated to West Africa from the area of Nubia about the time that the depictions of dugout-looking boats with sails were being made there. Also, it is known that the largest dugouts used on West African rivers have one or more masts flying square, reed-mat "insignia," or "flags." Do we see in these masts and mat "flags" the vestiges of masts and sails? Did the sails shrink because they would prove relatively useless for river navigation, but were they retained in miniature because of tradition?

Indirect support of this theory can be found in artistic representations of apparently native craft with sails, which were drawn by Portuguese artists. The shape of the sails in these paintings does not conform with rigs used in Portugal in the late 1400s and early 1500s, but they do look like Egyptian ones of the Sixth Dynasty. The hull form appears to be similar to that of Egyptian ships of that same period, although the Egyptian ships were planked and these West African craft would have been carved from a single log. It appears likely that West

Africans would not have had to paddle to the New World, but could have sailed there—and perhaps back—at any time from 1000 B.C. until shortly before European discovery.

As is the case with other aspects of West African history, nothing is known for certain about maritime achievements. We don't know what sort of boats or what level of nautical sophistication the West Africans boasted in 1000 B.C. and we are unlikely ever to know. A humid tropical climate ensures the rapid destruction of things made of wood or reed, like boats and rafts. All that can be said is that, when the Europeans came to West Africa in the mid-fifteenth century, the peoples of the coast had huge dugout canoes and sewn plank boats as well as reed boats closely resembling Heyerdahl's *Ra I* and *Ra II*. All three types of water craft are still in common use in West Africa.

But we may speculate about the type of vessels the West Africans might have used in 1000 B.C. and speculate about their degree of nautical sophistication. As a guide we can refer to the maritime achievements of another people, the ancient Peruvians, who had roughly the same cultural level and similar opportunity for seafaring offered by an oceanic coastline.

Peru, unlike West Africa, has a hot and dry coastline, which has been compared to a moonscape by more than one writer because of seemingly endless vistas of fine sand, bare rock and almost total lack of any sort of vegetation. A hostile environment for men, the climate has proved exceptionally kind to artifacts. Preserved in the Peruvian sand are articles that have allowed archeologists to reconstruct a fairly complete picture of the material culture of coastal Peruvians from the very primitive fisher folk of 700 B.C. to the splendor of the Incas 2,000 years later. And from even the earliest and most primitive levels of coastal occupation the Peruvian sand has yielded evidence of an astonishing nautical virtuosity.

It has only been within the past two decades that Western scholars have begun to recognize Peruvian maritime artifacts for what they are and to accept audacious ancient Peruvian voyaging far out into the Pacific. Thor Heyerdahl has almost single-handedly been responsible for this re-evaluation. In following Heyerdahl's research into the maritime achievements of ancient Andeans, we may be able to gain some reasonable idea about what the ancient West Africans could have achieved.

"No American people was ever a maritime people," pronounced

Adalbert von Chamisse in 1842. A century later, scholars were still saying the same thing:

> Altogether, we are justified in concluding that in Peruvian navigation prior to the Spanish conquest, the balsa-log raft, with sails, deck house, and cargo-space, was the least contemptible and the least inefficient type of craft known. This, admittedly, is faint praise; but, in view of the facts, it is the best that can be given to the boat-building art of those singularly unmarine-minded people, the ancient Andeans.[6]

The noted Americanist, S. K. Lothrop, writing in 1932 (*Aboriginal Navigation off the West Coast of South America*) claimed that the balsa raft "absorbs water rapidly and loses its buoyancy completely after a few weeks. Owing to this characteristic, it was necessary to take the *Jangada* (balsa raft) apart at intervals, haul the logs ashore, and there allow them to dry out completely." Heyerdahl notes: "Lothrop concluded that the balsa raft was unfit for oversea voyages, and that it could not travel as far as to the Pacific islands, not even to the Galapagos group a few hundred miles offshore."[7]

"Experts" like Lothrop were talking nonsense. The true facts about balsa rafts had been recorded long before by the real experts, those seamen who had seen Inca rafts under sail in the early days of the Conquest. All agreed on the outstanding qualities of the balsa rafts and all considered the Indians to be great mariners. From Sáamanos we learn that an Inca raft overhauled by Pizarro's expedition "carried masts and yards of very fine wood, and cotton sails in the same shape and manner as on our own ships. It had very good rigging of the said henequen, which is like hemp, and some mooring stones for anchors formed like grindstones."[8] Andagoya insisted that the henequen rope possessed by the Peruvian Indians was "stronger than that of Spain"[9] and they had "excellent cotton canvas" for sails. De Lizarraga wrote: "These Indians are great mariners; they have large rafts of light timber with which they navigate the ocean, and while fishing they remain many leagues out at sea." Cobo adds: "These rafts navigate the ocean by means of sail and paddles, and some are so large that they are easily able to carry fifty men."[10]

As late as 1825, W. B. Stevenson wrote about surviving Indian rafts that were so large that their deckhouses consisted of four or five rooms. The rafts were observed "beating up against the wind and current a distance of four degrees of latitude, having on board five or six quintals (25-30 tons) of goods as a cargo, besides a crew of Indians and their provisions." In 1840, George Blaxland wrote that he met a group of Indians on the island of Lobos de Afuera off the coast of South America, who were preparing their raft for the return voyage to the mainland sixty miles distant:

> They had been absent from their Native Village three weeks, and were about to return with a Cargo of Dried Fish, the Family consisted of Nine persons, with a Number of Dogs and all their goods and chattels. . . . The Vessel I was in, a schooner of 40 tons sailed for the same place in company, and it was surprising to see the manner the raft held the wind, going at the rate of four or five knots an hour; we kept together for some time and arrived the next day within a few hours of each other.

Yet, in spite of these eyewitness accounts by seamen, Hutchinson in his *Anthropology of Prehistoric Peru* dismissed the balsa raft as "a floating bundle of corkwood." And as late as 1945, Peter Buck could write: "The South American Indians had neither the vessels nor the navigating ability to cross the open ocean space between their shores and the nearest Polynesian islands."

The truth of the matter is that the South American Indians discovered and settled the Polynesian islands long before the "Polynesians" arrived there. They sailed to the islands on their balsa rafts and reed boats and returned to the mainland against 4,000 miles of contrary winds and currents. The Incas, not the Spanish, first discovered the Polynesian islands, just as the Incas, and not Dutch Admiral Jacob Roggeveen, first discovered Easter Island. In fact, the Indians of Peru gave the Spanish precise sailing directions to Easter Island from Callao: sail 600 leagues west-southwest of Callao, pass a small island to port (Sala-y-Gomez) and sight Easter Island soon after on the starboard bow. Unfortunately, Gallego, the pilot of the first Mendaña expedition, chose not to follow these accurate directions and turned due west before traveling 600 leagues. Thus he missed Easter Island and headed into the heart of Polynesia. He missed these islands too, because for some reason he later altered

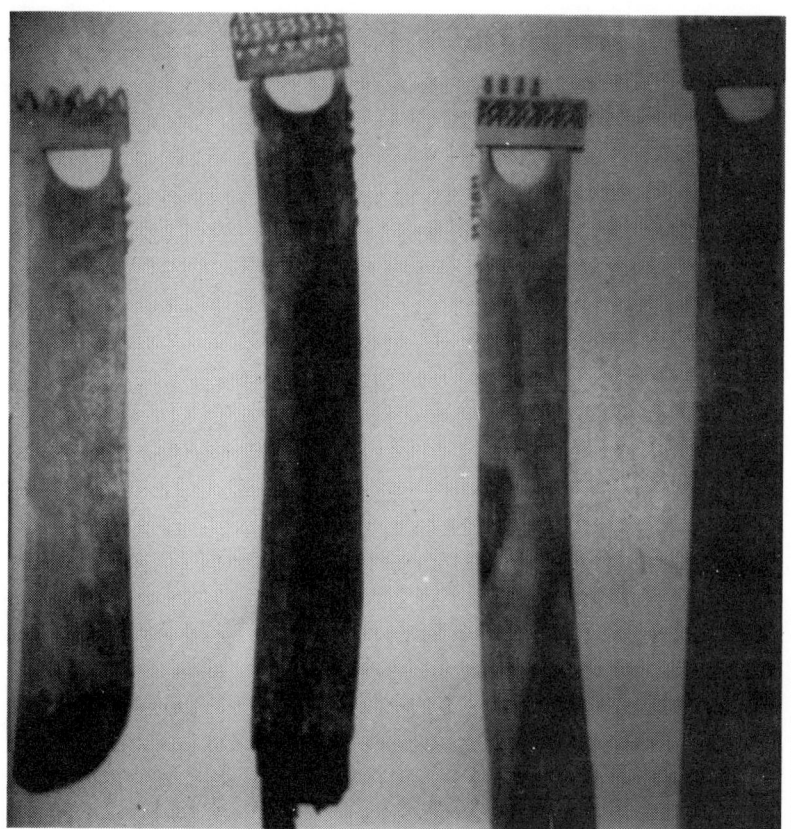

Guara boards *like these are a common find in Peruvian coastal graves. Although it is now known that guara boards are leeboards for balsa rafts, they were originally identified as "agricultural implements" by western archeologists.*

course to the northwest and the ship passed between the Tuamotu Group and the Marquesas without sighting either.

Modern Western experts simply ignored the facts because of prejudice. They refused to accept the evidence that was before their eyes in all the standard references of the Conquest, because they could not accept that a raft was a proper seagoing craft. In the European tradition, one must be "in," rather than "on," a vessel, and "real" ships are built up from a "true keel" and frames.

As everyone knows, Heyerdahl was able to prove the maritime abilities of the Peruvian Indians by building a replica raft and by sailing it 4,000 miles to Polynesia. This feat had important academic repercussions in that it was the beginning of the

Heyerdahl's *Ra I* *being steered with paddles lashed vertically on the side of the hull after steering oars broke off the coast of Africa. Using the long Egyptian paddles* guara-fashion, *the papyrus boat could be sailed across the wind, but not actually to windward.*

end of the myth: that Polynesia had been settled from Indonesia. For, by proving that the Indians could have reached Polynesia with his *Kon-Tiki* voyage, Heyerdahl forced open a psychological door in the hitherto closed minds of modern experts. With newly opened eyes, these experts began to look at the evidence for what it was: Polynesia had been first settled and discovered by Indians from South America about 500 A.D. There was a subsequent infusion of population from the Northwest Coast of North America and together these populations formed the "Polynesians."

[*Kon-Tiki*] proved to be an exceedingly seaworthy craft, perfectly adapted for carrying heavy cargoes in the open and unsheltered ocean. Of all the outstanding qualities none surprised and impressed us more than its safety and sea-

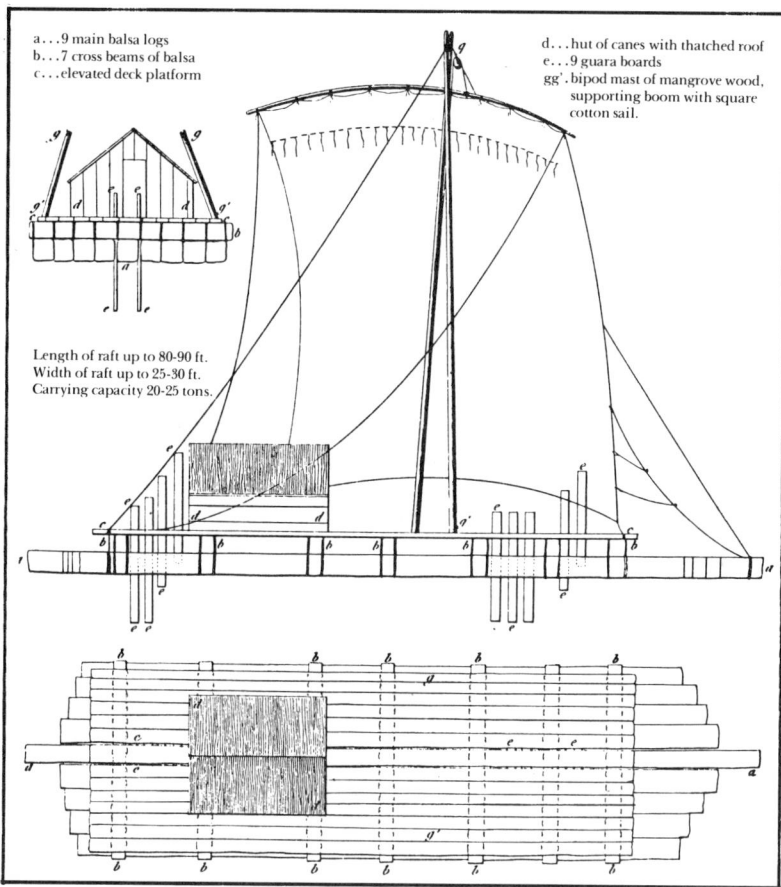

The building principles of the aboriginal balsa raft of Northwestern South America. Plan made in Guayaquil by Paris (1841-43).

Guara boards have been found in great numbers at Peruvian and Chilean sites. Guara boards are exactly like the "dagger boards" fitted to modern sailing dinghies; however, the guaras not only prevent leeway, they can also be used for steering the raft.

worthiness in all weather conditions at sea. Next to its unique ability to ride the waves came perhaps its carrying capacity, which, however, was no surprise, since balsa rafts capable of carrying up to thirty tons or more were described by the early Spaniards.

It was perhaps unrealistic to expect a modern crew of landlubbers to learn in just one voyage how to steer the raft as the

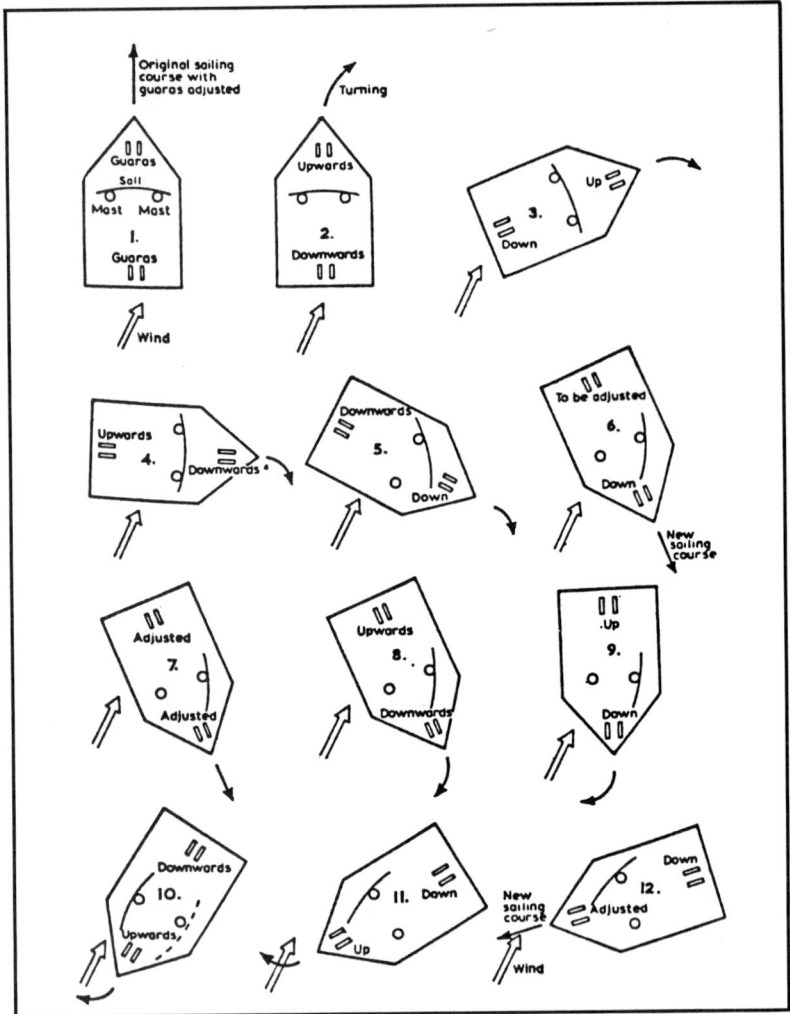

Guara Navigation

Incas had done, and all of Heyerdahl's attempts to sail to windward were unsuccessful in that first passage:

> However, . . . in 1953 the experiment was renewed. Mr. Emilio Estrada of Guayaquil kindly arranged for the building of a smaller test raft constructed like *Kon-Tiki* of nine logs lashed together and covered by a bamboo deck. Likewise, for navigation, a square sail was hoisted on its usual bipod mast in native fashion, and similarly six *guaras* were

inserted between the logs, two in the extreme bow and two in the stern. . . . Our suspicion was verified: a correct interplay between the handling of the sail and the *guaras* fore and aft enabled us, after some experimentation, to tack against contrary wind, and even to sail back to the exact spot where we had set off. The *guara* method of steering a raft was astonishing through its simplicity and effectiveness.[12]

It may be added here that although the Incas employed cotton sails of a square shape, the edges of the sail were sewn to a strong "bolt-rope" so that the edge of the sail could be sheeted stiffly at an angle to the wind, as shown in the diagram of *guara* navigation drawn after Heyerdahl.

The Peruvian balsa raft was undoubtedly safer at sea than early Spanish vessels. Not only did the raft ride waves better, but also any water taken aboard immediately ran out between the logs as there was no hull to be filled with breaking seas. The raft was also incomparably better to windward than sixteenth-century European vessels. Indeed, as late as the 1800s the raft's windward performance was compared to that of a pilot boat. The only advantage the Spaniards seem to have enjoyed was faster downwind sailing. Early accounts speak of the rafts being "overhauled" by caravels, no doubt due to the greater spread of canvas on Spanish vessels.

The advantages of the balsa raft were shared in large measure by the two papyrus boats that Heyerdahl later made. It is true that *Ra I* began to break up, and that the boat-building skill of the Badumas of the Lake Chad area proved inadequate to the task of crossing the Atlantic. Yet, it must be borne in mind that the 1969 voyage of *Ra I* began at Safi in Morocco and the boat covered some 3,000 miles before being abandoned. Even though it had been constructed incorrectly (because the Egyptian representations of reed boats had been partly misunderstood), *Ra I* sailed much further than the distance separating Cape Verde from South America.

Ra II, which successfully completed the crossing from Safi to Barbados in 1970, was built by Indians of Lake Titicaca, where reed sailing boats are still in daily use. Both papyrus boats exhibited impressive stability and wave-riding ability, great carrying capacity and gave the crew a feeling of complete security even in the worst storms.

Again, Heyerdahl did not succeed in making either papyrus boat steer to windward, even with *guaras*. I believe that this, too, should be attributed to inexperience with the craft—after all, no one had built and sailed an ocean-going reed vessel for about 2,000 years. Heyerdahl lashed his *guaras* to the sides of the reed boats fore and aft, but they could not work effectively as leeboards, for, unlike the cracks between the logs of a raft, the sides of these boats were curved; the paddles lashed to the side as *guaras* therefore cut through the water at an angle to the direction of travel rather than directly in line with it.

I believe that a reed boat can be steered to windward if the paddles are inserted between reed bundles so that they are kept parallel to the center-line of the boat, just as *guaras* are parallel to the longitudinal axis of balsa rafts. I think that the pointed paddle, besides yielding the "high aspect ratio" efficiency of leeboards, may also have evolved in order to make it easier for the paddles to be pushed downward between reed bundles and into the water beneath the boat.

Alternatively, the same type of paddle could be lashed successfully to the gunwale of a dugout because, except at extreme bow and stern, the sides of a dugout are straight and parallel rather than continuously curved like the depictions of papyrus rafts. Paddles lashed to a dugout's sides would not cut the water at an angle to the boat's direction of movement; they would serve effectively as leeboards for a windward-sailing dugout (just as similar "kits" can be purchased today that allow canoes to be sailed into the wind).

In speculating upon the vessels that the black Africans of Cape Verde possessed, we may be led astray by enthusiasm and imagination. But we may be led as far astray by prejudice. Western ethnocentricity allowed our scholars to ignore the capabilities of even the most primitive-appearing craft—lashed logs and lashed bundles of reeds—until Heyerdahl opened our eyes with his experiments of 1948, 1953, 1969 (*Ra I*) and 1970 (*Ra II*). Then, not only were such basic vessels shown to be adequate, but in some measure superior to European craft of Lief Ericsson's and Columbus' time—and, perhaps, superior in some respects to vessels of our own time. Even when *Ra I* was breaking up off Barbados, the crew could watch from their floating "mattress" how alarmingly the rescue vessel rolled in the sea; they could still seriously debate whether they were better off to remain on what papyrus bundles were still held together with rope or to venture aboard a modern boat that looked thoroughly unsafe. All the *Ra I* crew voted to continue the voyage; the decision to abandon the boat was Heyerdahl's alone. He knew that basic mistakes of conception and construction had been made with *Ra I* and knew, therefore, that any further risk was needless. Another papyrus boat could be constructed, building on the lessons already learned, that would cross the Atlantic easily. And so he proved with *Ra II*.

If we can so seriously underestimate the virtues of such primitive craft, is it safe to denigrate the sailing abilities of much more sophisticated dugouts or sewn planked boats?

Aside from hints in the sails and paddles of early Egyptian-African vessels, one more detail, preserved in the earliest art, indicates that they possessed windward ability. In the next chapter, using the artistic evidence and speculation, and guided by the unsuspected efficiency of even more primitive vessels, I will offer a possible reconstruction of a West African ocean-going vessel of approximately 1000 B.C.

7

Black Ships of the Bronze Age

Exactly what kind of boats are represented in the Nubian rock drawings of 3000 B.C.? We see curiously curved hulls driven by paddlers and, sometimes, by sails. Egyptologists like Sir Flinders Petrie believe that all these drawings represent papyrus boats. But naval architecture historian Björn Landström thinks that some of the curved hulls shown on the rocks and on Nagadeh II pottery suggest either a basic three-plank vessel or even larger boats that are variations on the three-plank concept. The planks would have been sewn together with rope; the larger versions must have boasted some interior framing in order to hold them together. Some of the hulls show high vertical extensions of bow and stern. Without exception, all the hulls showing sails have either this vertical extension front and back or a deeply curved profile.

Whether the rock drawings show dugout canoes or papyrus boats or planked-and-sewn vessels, I believe that either a deeply curved hull or high bow and stern extensions were necessary, but only for a long, narrow vessel designed to sail into the wind. Here's why:

Heyerdahl has said that these up-curving bows and sterns were designed to take the waves of ocean voyaging. Speaking of Cheops' ship, Heyerdahl writes: "Its gracefully curved hull with elegantly upthrust and extremely high bow and stern had all the characteristic features found only in seagoing vessels, specially shaped to ride breakers and towering waves."[1]

Yes, of course. The high sterns and bows would certainly part the force of large waves, but they had a more important function: to provide positive stability in the event of a knock-down or near-capsize in high or even in moderate waves.

Today's naval architects provide sufficient weight of ballast on the base of the keel to lever the boat from a knock-down back up to a vertical position. But the same effect can be obtained

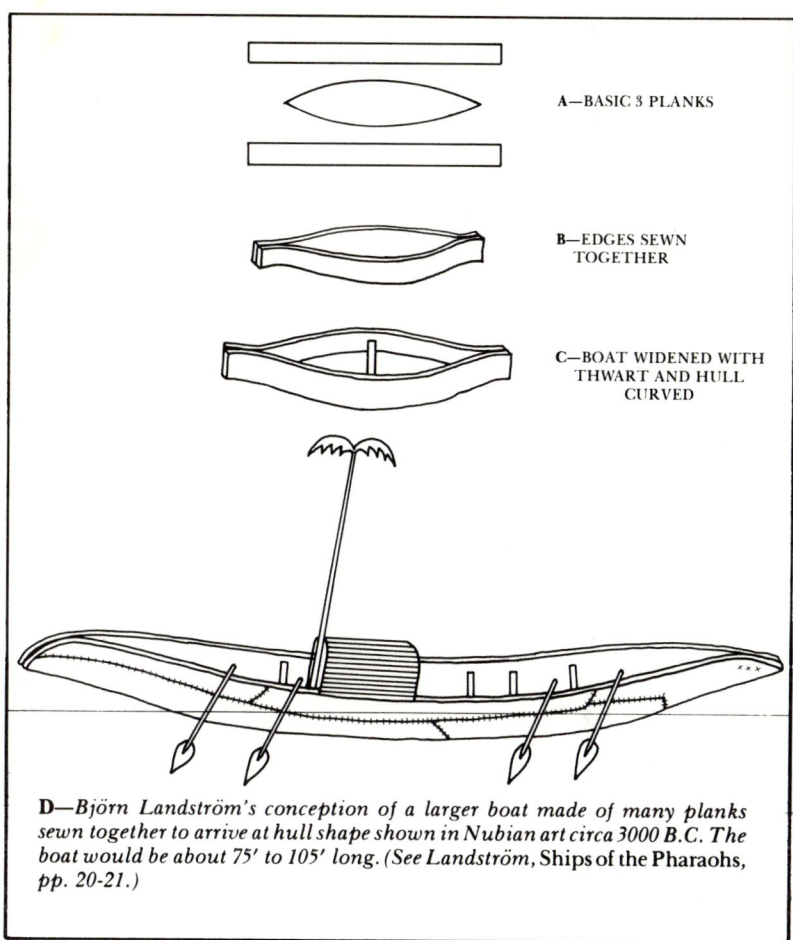

D—*Björn Landström's conception of a larger boat made of many planks sewn together to arrive at hull shape shown in Nubian art circa 3000 B.C. The boat would be about 75' to 105' long. (See Landström,* Ships of the Pharaohs, *pp. 20-21.)*

if the bow and stern are upthrust and made of buoyant material: the lighter, upthrust sections will rise, forcing the heavier section, the base, down into the water. A glance at the diagram will show that, although a vessel with a high and buoyant bow and stern can be blown over so that it lies sideways in the water, it cannot capsize or turn completely over. As long as the boat is relatively small, it can be righted by its crew.

Boats designed to sail only downwind may also be accidentally capsized, of course, if the wind suddenly gusts from any direction but astern, but this would occur rarely. However, knock-down would be a rather frequent occurrence on a boat designed to sail into the wind, especially if the hull was rather long and narrow. Yet as long as the danger could be limited to

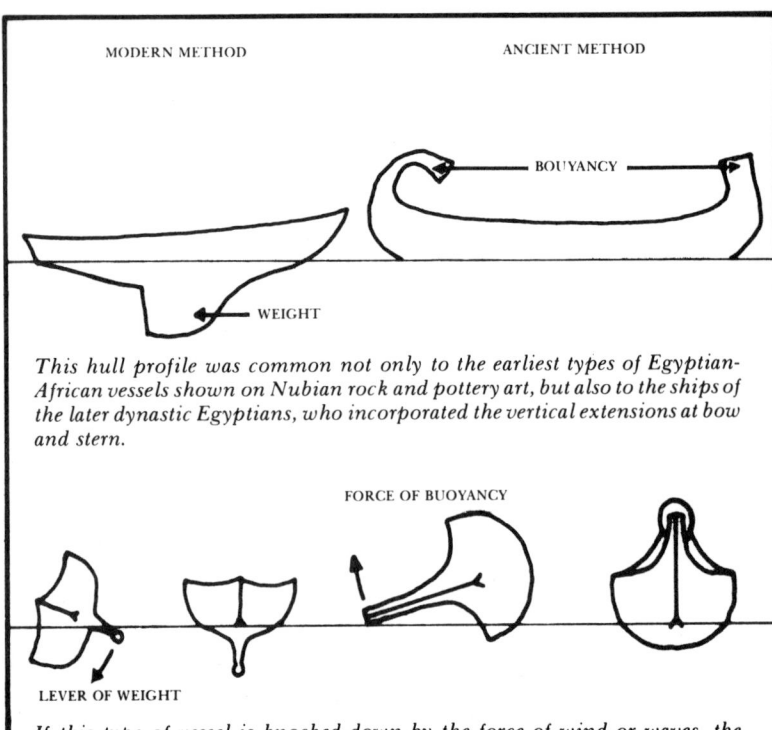

This hull profile was common not only to the earliest types of Egyptian-African vessels shown on Nubian rock and pottery art, but also to the ships of the later dynastic Egyptians, who incorporated the vertical extensions at bow and stern.

If this type of vessel is knocked down by the force of wind or waves, the buoyant bow and stern extensions prevent the vessel from capsizing in the water. A small boat could be righted by swimming crewmen pushing up on the bow and stern extensions; a small amount of ballast would assist the procedure in a larger vessel. Modern design incorporates heavy ballast on a deep keel to prevent capsize.

knock-down rather than complete capsizing, and provided there was some provision for the boat to be righted easily in the water by its crew, there was no reason for this event to be a catastrophe. Even the cargo, if lashed securely; would not be lost. Therefore, it seems reasonable that positive stability would only be built into boats used for windward sailing.

I think that it is at least possible that the very first sailing boats were dugouts whose hulls were not curved, but straight as the tree from which they were made. The first vertical extensions at bow and stern would have been separate pieces. Very possibly, they were removable, and would be added only when sailing was attempted, as they would not be necessary when the boat was intended to be moved by paddle-power alone. In time, perhaps, the hull itself became increasingly curved and the vertical extensions became smaller until, finally, the separate extensions disappeared altogether and only curved hulls remained. No one knows how long such a hypothetical evolution would take or what stages it would pass through. It is certainly not clear from the rock drawings and ships shown on pottery of about 3000 B.C.

In my opinion, however, almost all sailing ships of the ancient world show vestiges of this evolution. The upcurving sterns and the upward bow extensions of many ancient ships were not merely decorative, nor were they only memorials to earlier "papyriform" vessels. They were also functional, preventing a knock-down from becoming a capsize. Although useful to any sailing vessel on occasion, these vertical extensions of bow and stern would be vital for boats that sailed across the wind or somewhat to windward.

Although it cannot be proved, these high bows and sterns, together with the shape of the paddles and the use of mat sails, convince me that Egyptian-African boats depicted from predynastic times in Nubia could move to windward, and would have been sailed on lakelike expansions of the Nile that have subsequently dried up.

It remains to be determined whether these boats were made of papyrus, hollowed logs or sewn planks. Some were unquestionably papyrus, but some hulls could have been of other material. Most experts are agreed that the first boat was a dugout, but Björn Landström is of the opinion that the Nubia of 3000 B.C., though parkland-savannah, probably lacked trees of sufficient size to make dugouts of the dimensions suggested by the number of paddles—and thus paddlers—shown in rock and pottery art. Landström offers the speculation that boats, more or less in imitation of dugouts, were made of planks sewn together with rope after the three-plank mode of boat-building. "The smaller craft can have been 25 m. long, with a beam of 2.5 m. One could call it a canoe. The larger was perhaps 35 m. long, and 3 m. in the beam."[2]

If the sewn-boat technique existed, it is possible that some of these Nubians brought it with them in their migrations to West Africa. But it seems obvious that once among trees of suitable size, they would gradually and inevitably revert to the building of dugouts. Landström readily admits that the sewn boat would have been "inevitably leaky" and not very strong. People would naturally turn from it if a better method of boat-building was at hand. But the basic design we see in the Nubian draw-

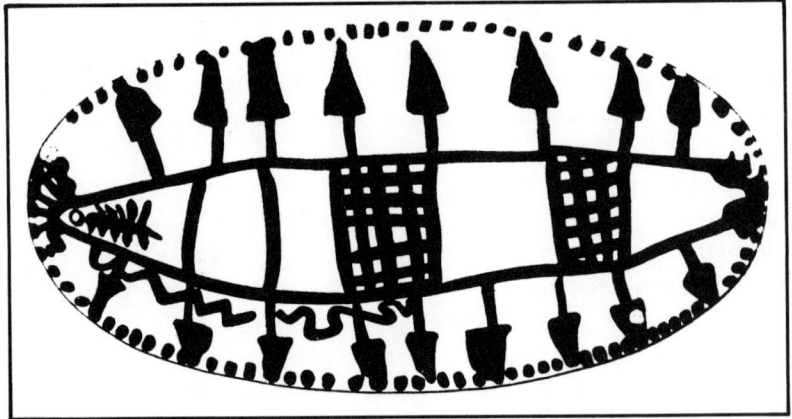

Primitive, oared river boat *in bird's-eye view, circa 3500 B.C. Top view of boat. Note the shape of the paddles.*

ings probably would have been retained.

I have ventured a reconstruction of a West African sea-going dugout of about 1000 B.C., approximately the time when bronze had just been established south of the Sahara and the cultures of the New World were beginning to develop. My reconstruction is entirely speculative, based upon interpretations of the Nubian drawings and the knowledge that people from Nubia migrated to West Africa between 3000 and 1000 B.C. It is of the very earliest type of West African sea-going canoe, which would have been in use very shortly after Nubian migrants trickled into the area of West Africa and Cape Verde.

With a reasonably skilled crew, such a craft could make a trade-wind passage to America with little difficulty and, just possibly, sail back on a broad tack against the northeast trades, be paddled through the doldrums, and return to Cape Verde.

To my knowledge, no West African canoe of this period has actually been discovered and there are no artistic representations yet found in West Africa that show boats of this time. Neither are there early European or Arab artistic representations of canoes of this shape. However, several Portuguese and other European paintings do show that dugouts with sharply curved hulls resembling Egyptian boats of the dynastic periods existed much later than 3000 B.C.

In my view, the Nubian migrants to both West Africa and Egypt would have naturally developed their craft along the same lines: the straight hull and vertical extensions would

Nubian rock drawings of long-hulled vessels. *These could be dugouts, papyrus rafts or sewn-plank boats.*

gradually be modified into a more smoothly curving hull, but sometimes they would still retain vestiges of these ancient vertical appendages. And this is, in fact, what we seem to see in the evolution of Egyptian boats and what may be reasonably inferred from later European depictions of African canoes with a curved hull shape.

Doubtless the stem and stern vertical extensions would be carved and, indeed, the Nubian vase painting of a similar craft illustrated here does show a figurehead, possibly a bird, surmounting the stempiece. One might argue that I have placed the mast too far aft—that the Nubian craft has a mast definitely forward of amidships, and that a mast placed so far forward would suggest downwind capability only. However, I think the artist who drew this vessel on the vase is trying to give us a perspective of the boat moving away from the viewer. This is suggested by the angle of the boat's hull. If so, the exact position of the mast may also be distorted as this drawing is not a simple profile.

This is how I imagine a black African ship of the early sub-Saharan Bronze Age to have been. Perhaps fifty feet in length,

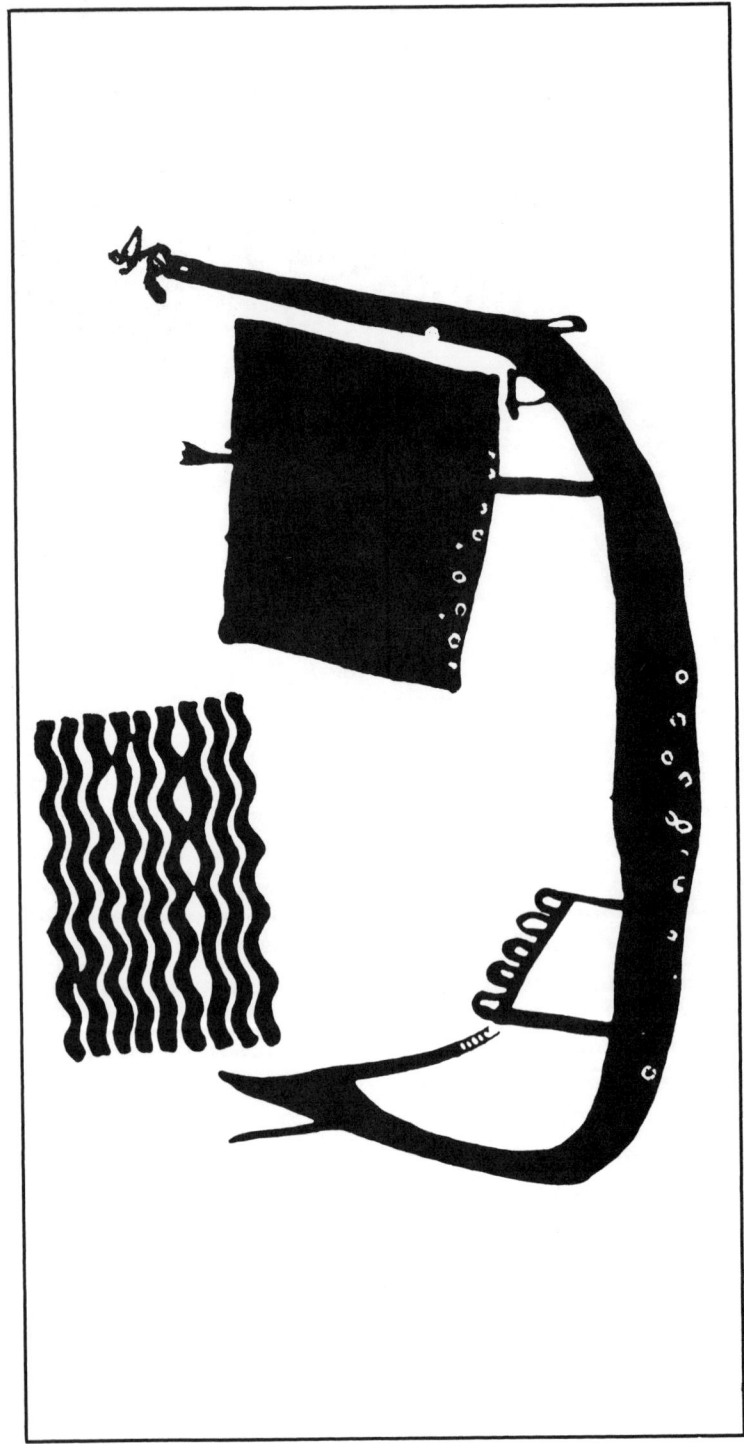

Earliest representation of a sail, *circa 3100 B.C., from Nagadeh pottery. Is this a papyrus raft, a dugout or a sewn-plank boat?*

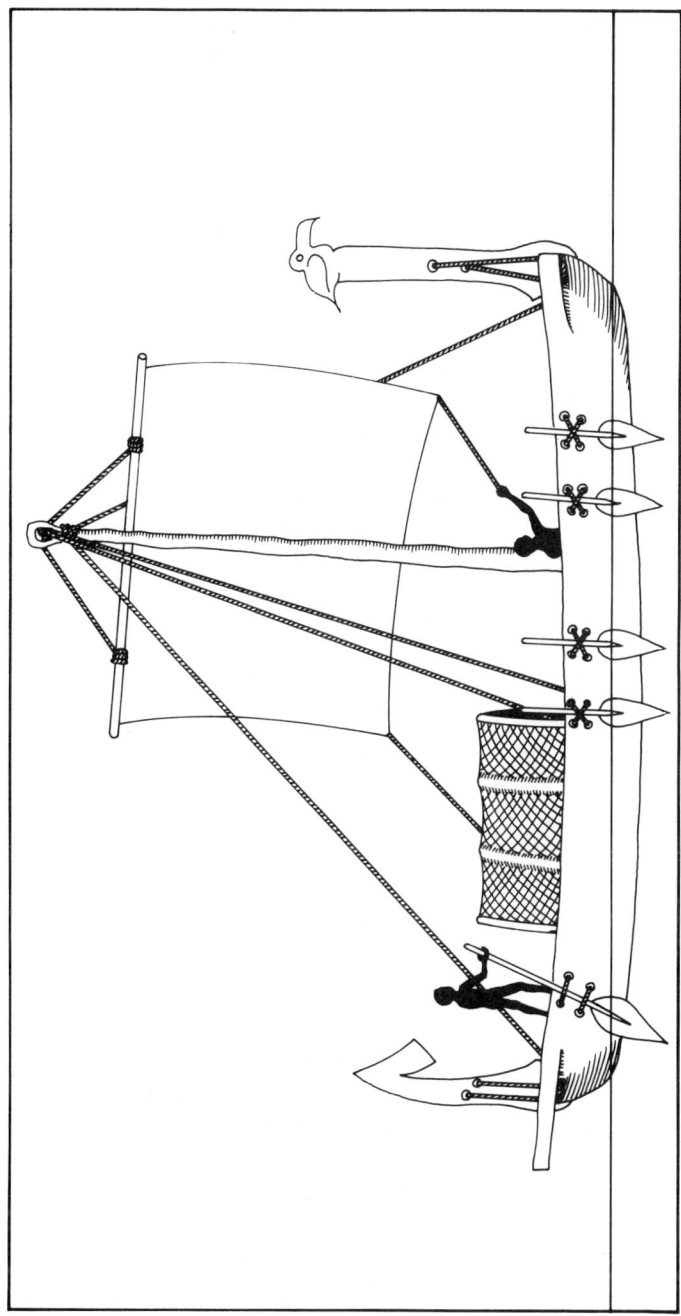

Hypothetical Reconstruction of a Sea-going Canoe
Based on Nubian art of circa 3000 B.C., the canoe depicted here is about 45' to 50' in length and carries a crew of about fifteen people.

six to eight feet in beam and about four feet deep from gunwale amidships to the "keel" or bottom of the boat. The sail might be 225 to 300 square feet of mat or cotton, since it is known that the West Africans of that time had domesticated cotton and were weaving. The deckhouse would have been a wickerwork or woven mat shelter with a rounded top, much like the deckhouses represented in the predynastic art. The cordage would have been of palm-leaf fiber, like the "rope" the Baduma make today in the Lake Chad region to hold the papyrus reed bundles of their *kadays* together.

This vessel would have been large, but by no means as large as the biggest dugouts described by early Europeans on the Guinea Coast. Used primarily for offshore fishing or for coastal trading in bronze, cotton or gold, such a ship would have a crew of ten to fifteen men and carry perhaps four to six tons of cargo. Downwind, the craft would be very swift. It might sail within five to seven points of the wind, making considerable leeway while doing so, and it would be tricky to handle except by a thoroughly experienced crew. The vertical extensions at bow and stern would be thick planks set in sockets cut into the dugout and lashed in place with rope.

This ship is, in fact, not so very different from the famous pitch-smeared "black ships" of the *Iliad* and the *Odyssey* in the early days of our own Bronze Age. In fact, although some or even most of the Homeric ships were built of frames and planks, Björn Landström has suggested that some of the ships drawn up on the beach at Troy were dugouts. Sailing off the coast of Africa, these black African ships would have met a Homeric rosy-fingered dawn no less swiftly than the famous ships from Sandy Pylos; and there is no reason to believe that the black mariners rode the billows of the wine-dark sea with any less competence or any less joy of adventure than crafty Odysseus and his shipmates. And if the bird figurehead on the stempiece looks primitive and barbaric to our eyes, we should remember that the ships of the Myrmidons at Troy boasted figureheads no less primitive and barbaric, carved in the likeness of an ant.

It was in ships such as this, I believe, that black Africans crossed to the New World, stumbled into the mouth of the Amazon, and followed it inland to the eastern foothills of the Andes where the first Amerindian culture began and where the influence of the African language Mandinga has been determined. And what would be more natural for these African visitors than sailing and paddling up a tropical river? At home they navigated up the Senegal, the Gambia, the Niger. The Amazon would hold no terrors for them.

By the first years of the Christian era, and possibly long before, black Africans had reached the southern coast of Yucatan. To do this, they sailed farther along the coast of South America, entered the Caribbean and crossed to Yucatan or, once established in modern Colombia, Brazil and Venezuela, followed a river down to the sea to reach the land of the Olmecs.

I'm inclined to the notion that these people followed a river. It may have been the Orinoco, because it is the largest river that flows from the South American mainland and the eastern highlands into the Caribbean. However, the Orinoco takes something of a detour before reaching the Caribbean, so other rivers—notably the Magdalena and the Cauca—would have served the Africans better. This smaller river system drains an area of Colombia and Venezuela where the Muisca culture—perhaps the forerunner of Chavin itself—flourished, and these rivers join to enter the sea west of Maracaibo on the Caribbean shore of Venezuela. From there it is but a short hop or coastal voyage to the Olmec lands.

It is on these eastern slopes that we must focus our interest. The Amazon provided the Africans with a highway from the Atlantic, while the Orinoco, Magdalena and Cauca river systems provided a way by which culture begun in these foothills could radiate northward to the Olmecs and eastward, by smaller Pacific-flowing streams, to the lands of the Chavin culture and eventually to the Incas.

It is in these foothills that we find African linguistic traces and artistic parallels. They represent the shortest route by which the African bottle gourd could have reached the Pacific and Mexico, and encompass the area where the very earliest Spanish river-explorers found plantations of African plantain domesticated by the Indians. This is also the place where cotton was probably first domesticated in the New World and subsequently carried north and east.

Before leaving this speculative section, I would like to mention something about rafts. Although I think it most probable that black Africans crossed the Atlantic in large sailing dugout canoes, there remains the possibility that they used rafts instead. Certainly, any such people, living as they did in an area offering exceptional raft-building material, would have known how to build rafts for use on rivers. (Today the Sobo of the Niger delta use small rafts for fishing.) Even if they preferred handy dugouts for ordinary purposes—and transatlantic travel—knowledge of raft-building would have been brought by black African visitors to the New World.

When we consider the sea-going rafts of the Incas, we see the use of rafts for ocean voyaging as a unique indigenous culture trait. Yet, it may have been an acquired trait, like cotton and bottle-gourd domestication and the smelting and working of precious metals. It is at least thought-provoking, therefore, that the earliest representations of rafts are found among the riverine cultures of the eastern Andean slopes. These people obviously used rafts on the major rivers. Now it may be that the idea of rafts is something that would occur naturally to any people in proximity to both large trees and water. But perhaps not. The great virtue of a raft is that it carries a relatively large amount of cargo; but large-scale cargo-carrying would be required only with the development of some culture and attendant commerce or trade.

It is at least possible that, along with some evolved culture, black Africans brought the knowledge and tradition of making rafts to carry the products of trade that "culture" inevitably produces. Dugouts would still have been handier for small traffic on the rivers and would doubtless have been known by the Indians before any visitors arrived. Large dugouts, like those known to have been made in West Africa, would have had their advantages at sea. But it seems that rafts would be of use on large rivers only when the flow of cargoes, inspired by "culture" and trading, reached a certain point. Perhaps, after arriving in the foothills of the eastern Andean slopes, the initial black African visitors inspired both culture and the use of riverine rafts.

We find ancient representations of rafts of some size among the cultures of ancient Colombia. It is possible that the raft-building technique was passed on to the Pacific coast, like much else, by these inland cultures. And the Pacific peoples, lacking material for huge dugouts suitable for seafaring, developed instead the sea-going raft from balsa logs. Balsa is too soft to be hollowed out into dugouts, and too soft to make a rope-sewn craft of any strength. Although balsa logs come in straight lengths of great diameter, about the only thing that can be done with them is to make rafts.

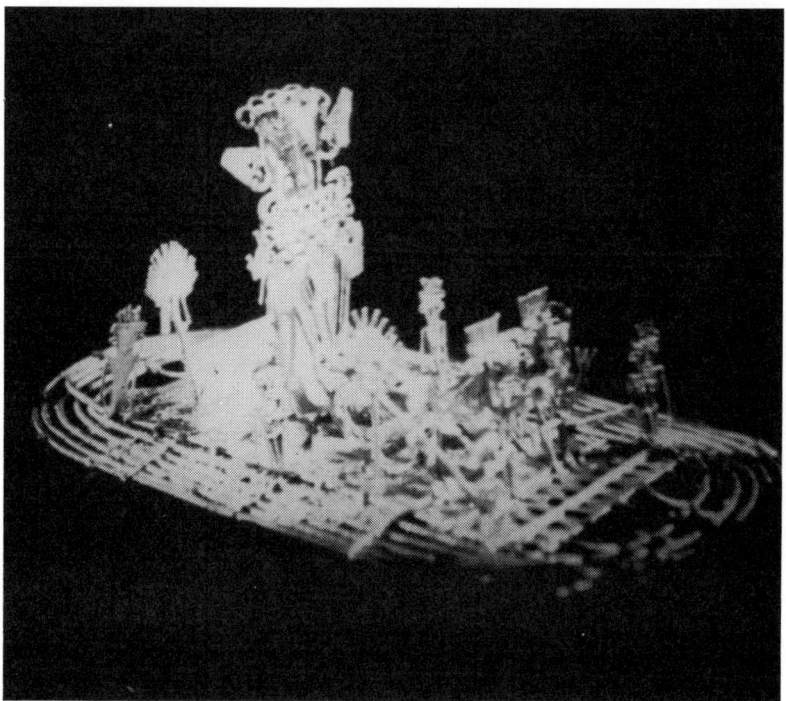

Gold raft model *from Colombia shows chief and crew aboard. Upper Amazon basin.*

The idea of a raft that could be used for true oceanic voyaging may have come to the Peruvians from the inland use of rafts on river systems, which, in turn, may have been previously dictated by the need to carry more cargo than a dugout could manage. Also, a large raft is obviously easier to make than a large dugout and the logs themselves may constitute part of the cargo. The sudden appearance of rafts in ancient Colombia may well have been inspired by a sudden upsurge in trade. Both the trade and the idea of using rafts may have been initiated by West African visitors.

Not only could black Africans have brought the knowledge of making log rafts for carrying heavy cargoes, they could also have brought the knowledge of making reed rafts for the same purpose. The knowledge of reed rafts would have been of less general applicability since reeds with a sponge-like interior and hard, waterproof outer sheath are required. The Africans knew of papyrus in the Old World, but they would not encounter a reed of similar properties until reaching the

Andean uplands where the *totora* grows. Then the knowledge of reed raft-making could be put to use—as it was among the Incas and still is among the Aymara Indians of Bolivia.

However, even if black Africans could have brought the knowledge of log and reed raft-making for the purpose of carrying cargo, I'm inclined to believe that they made the Atlantic crossing itself by large dugout. This sort of watercraft seems to be most characteristic of tropical forested regions, and large dugouts exist now and were described by the earliest European accounts of West Africa. But if I am justified in my speculation that paddle shape, sail material, rock-drawings and hull shape all suggest that ancient Africans could sail into the wind, then the possibility should not be discounted that the principle of the *guara* evolved from knowledge brought to the New World by black Africans.

Anyone who has ever tried to paddle a raft will know that it is an exercise in frustration. Peruvian sailors would have quickly abandoned the paddle as a means of moving a raft without wind, and they would have had to modify the paddle-blade itself for use as a centerboard. The handle or "loom" of a paddle would simply revolve round and round if sandwiched between slippery curved logs. Therefore, the handle would have been shortened or removed and only the blade inserted between the cracks in a log raft. Eventually, the blade itself would be all that remained of the original paddle, and would be gradually modified.

Although learning how to sail a raft into the wind is a great feat, it is not an obvious one. The *guara* must have evolved from some people who first began to paddle watercraft and subsequently learned how to sail them by modifying their paddle into a long blade for use as a centerboard. Only then could the principle be understood well enough to be adapted to something as unlikely as a raft. I contend that we see the evolution of this principle in the sailing drawings of Nubia about 3000 B.C., and that this knowledge was brought to the New World by black Africans who first applied it to sea-going canoes and, possibly, to papyrus rafts. The Incas then adapted the principle further for use on their log rafts. The Incas may also have used *guaras* on their *totora*-reed boats just as I suggest the Africans used their pointed paddles on papyrus boats. It seems that a thread of navigating evolution leads from Nubia to Peru.

We do not know whether the black Africans came across the

Atlantic in dugouts, reed boats, log rafts or sewn-plank vessels. All are possible. My reconstruction of the large dugout is offered merely because it seems the most probable form of watercraft, considering the place and time, for ordinary daily use—and therefore the most probable vessel in which an inadvertent transatlantic journey would have been accomplished by black Africans.

8

The Evidence of Botany

Man has domesticated many plants and animals according to his need, and whenever possible, he has taken them with him on his migrations. Until the fifteenth century it seems that everyone's watercraft were too small to carry domesticated cattle from the Old World to the New—with perhaps one exception. It is written in some Icelandic sagas that Thorfinn Karlsefni brought a bull with him to Lief's Shelters in Vinland—which authorities place anywhere from Baffin Island to Florida. It is not recorded whether the Karlsefni expedition took the bull with them when they left Vinland, but it is known that the bellowing of this strange monster so frightened the *skraelings*—Indians or Inuit—that Karlsefni's small band was able to win many skirmishes though the Norsemen were greatly outnumbered.

Karlsefni's lone bull could not have begun a bovine dynasty in the New World; it was left to the Spanish to introduce domesticated cattle into the Americas. But animals smaller than cattle, and many food plants, seem to have traveled with man from the Old World to America and beyond, out into the Pacific, in pre-Colombian times. It is Heyerdahl's opinion, for instance, that Inca dogs, which have been found mummified, do not appear to have been domesticated from native American canines but resemble African and, specifically, Egyptian dogs. We will leave the experts to argue over that contention, but the situation is not so uncertain when it comes to domesticated plants. Some plants thriving in the New World when the Spaniards first came had crossed the Atlantic long before. At least one native American plant, the coconut palm, had managed to cross the Pacific and become established in Indonesia and as far west as Ceylon by the second century A.D.

There is still no agreement about the original homelands of some domesticated plants. However, three important plants cultivated in pre-Columbian America undoubtedly originated in the Old World—two of them in tropical Africa—and all three could have been brought by mariners from the Cape Verde region. It is unlikely that any of these plants could have crossed the ocean and established themselves without human assistance. The three domesticated varieties are: the bottle gourd, cotton and plantain.

Bottle Gourd

Sometimes also called a "calabash," the bottle gourd (*Lagenaria siceraria* or *vulgaris*) was not only cultivated in the New World when the Spanish arrived but also well established far out into the Pacific. The interior of the gourd may be eaten, but its principal use—from Africa to Polynesia—is as a container, especially a water vessel, once the interior has been cleaned and the hard outer rind has been dried. Obviously, mariners familiar with the bottle gourd would have been certain to carry this item of equipment with them to the Americas.

Being so useful, this plant has traveled widely. It was grown in Egypt and nearby areas by at least 2500 B.C. and had reached China and Indonesia about 100 B.C. Some—notably Buck—have argued that the gourd was brought to America from Indonesia across the Pacific; but now it is known that the gourd existed in the Americas long before it existed in Indonesia and long before there were any Polynesians to carry it across the Pacific. It appears that this plant traveled both east and west from its tropical African homeland, but the Pacific was the last region where it became established. Moreover, there is now overwhelming evidence that Peruvian mariners to Polynesia took the gourd with them about 500 A.D.

When did the South Americans obtain this gourd? Nordenskiold wrote in 1931:

> *Lagenaria* was even known to the very primitive fisher population of Africa where ancient graves have been studied by Uhle and the prominent botanist Skottsberg. These ancient fishermen had no pottery, and were unacquainted with the art of weaving. Thus it must have been very far back in time that *Lagenaria* was cultivated in America.[1]

The Arica graves can be dated about 700 B.C. or somewhat earlier.

Some have maintained that the calabash could have crossed the Atlantic on its own, using the equatorial currents and trade winds for passage, but Carter and Heyerdahl have shown that this would not have been possible. The bottle gourd, ironically, cannot withstand a lengthy soaking from the outside in a salt solution. Then, as Heyerdahl adds:

> The everpresent activity of pelagic crabs, boring crustaceans, and other surface patroling animals in these waters, as encountered and observed from the *Kon-Tiki* raft, would not permit any gourd to drift for thousands of miles without being perforated and damaged, if not entirely consumed, long before it could take root and flourish on a foreign shore.

This view is supported by Sauer who says: "It is in no sense a strand or marsh plant. The theory of its accidental dissemination involves, in addition to the undamaged transit of an ocean, a waiting agriculturalist who carried it in from the seashore to a suitable spot for cultivation."[2]

We may be assured that the bottle gourd came to America with the help of man, and probably came with mariners from the gourd's original homeland—tropical Africa.

Cotton

Cottons occur naturally in both the Old World and the New, but there are two distinctly different plants. All natural Old World cottons have thirteen small chromosomes, while wild American cottons have thirteen large chromosomes. Cotton domesticated by American cultures appear to be a hybrid of both, having twenty-six chromosomes—thirteen small and thirteen large.[3] The plant was probably domesticated first in the Old World at a very early date. Then:

> Suddenly, in a more recent time, but before the arrival of the Europeans, the same domesticated Old World cotton appeared in aboriginal America, where it was used by the leading New World culture-peoples to produce their own local 26-chromosomed cotton.[4]

Henri Lhote's work at Tassili revealed a rock drawing of a charioteer showing what may be a woven kilt on the human figure. It may be that the center of Old World cotton cultivation was originally in the Sahara, and refugees from increasing drought brought knowledge of cotton cultivation with them to their adopted havens. Cotton would then have come to West Africa at a very early date.

No one knows when cotton was first domesticated and woven by the West Africans of antiquity. Cotton production and fine weaving and dying are casually mentioned by the first Arabic writers on West Africa. This would lead to the conclusion that it was not considered remarkable, and that knowledge of cotton domestication and use had been long known among the black Africans when the Arabs came into contact with them.

"Cotton is apparently as ancient as the gourd in archeological sites of the New World. . . . All but one of the oldest mummy wrappings from Ancon and Supe were of cotton."[5] In North Peru, where the Chavin culture emerges, cotton is older than either pottery or maize.

Cotton was apparently carried to the Pacific by early Peruvian settlers in Polynesia. The cotton found on Pacific islands is not Old World cotton with thirteen small chromosomes, but the hybrid American cultivated cotton with twenty-six chromosomes.

Again, some experts have maintained that knowledge of cotton was brought to America via the Orient, from China and Indonesia. However, radiocarbon analysis shows that the earliest New World cottons date from about 1000 B.C., while cotton cultivation did not reach China and Indonesia until 700 A.D.[6]

One must conclude that cotton was brought to the Americas by people from Africa. Since its presence, along with the bottle gourd, exists before pottery in some areas, we may deduce that both cotton and the gourd were brought by people who, even if they knew pottery, did not rely upon it as a major culture-trait because back home they had materials better suited for most containers than ceramics. The only such people could have been blacks from tropical West Africa. Besides using the admirable bottle gourd as a domestic utensil, the black Africans developed an enduring tradition of fashioning jugs, pots and cups from wood. (This is not to say that they did not know pottery from the earliest times, but their plentiful timber meant that they were not restricted to the use of ceramics for domestic vessels.)

It is unthinkable that Mediterranean peoples of about 1000 B.C. would have brought cotton and the gourd without an emphasis on pottery. For by 1000 B.C. almost all domestic vessels in the Mediterranean were made of pottery.

It seems that much of the Mediterranean was deforested both by drought and human agency at a very early time. But clay and sand were plentiful and widespread, so the people logically turned to ceramics when domestic pots, bowls and other vessels were required. A very early pottery tradition was born in the eastern Mediterranean, which continued to be observed even when civilization seeped gradually into forested inland regions. But in tropical Africa a pottery tradition of comparable strength never developed because of the availability of alternative materials.

The fact that cotton and the bottle gourd but not pottery are found together in the New World suggests that the culture-bearers of these earliest migrations came from West Africa rather than from the Mediterranean.

Plantain

It has often been asserted that both the banana (*Musa paradisiaca*) and the plantain (*Musa normalis*) were brought to the New World from Cape Verde by the Spanish in 1516. This is certainly true of the banana, but doubtful for the plantain. During the first Spanish exploration of the eastern slopes of the Andes, conquistadors found plantations of plantains in Colombia and Venezuela where the great rivers take their sources. Could it be that, in only twenty-three years, American Indians managed to adopt the imported plant in Santo Domingo and transport it 2,000 miles into the interior of South America, and establish it in large areas, so that Orellana could report plantations of plantains in 1539?[7] It seems a little unlikely, particularly as cultivation of this species is initially difficult and slow because reproduction of the plant is by suckers. Several early writers specifically state that plantains were under native cultivation when the Spanish arrived, and plantain leaves have been identified from pre-Columbian burials.[8] It seems certain that the plantain was brought to the New World before Columbus, and this is a plant that must be helped across oceans by man.

Sarah Ruth Burman

arrival is not as noticeable as
the arrival of the Europeans is.

Even though the plant was widely traveled from the earliest times, the original home of the plantain is in tropical Africa. Only in tropical Africa has a bird—the plantain eater—evolved to specialize in feeding on this plant.

It is interesting that the Spanish and Portuguese brought the banana from Cape Verde. Very likely, the plantain had come to the New World from the same area, but much earlier. It is also interesting, as both Sauer and Heyerdahl note, that while the banana seems to be preferred by whites, the plantain is more used by the natives of the New World—and, one may observe, by the later black immigrants into the Caribbean.

Evidence offered by the bottle gourd, twenty-six-chromosome cotton and plantain seems to indicate that these tropical African plants were brought to the New World by men before Columbus. The most likely men to do this would have been the West Africans who shared their environment with these plants.

9
Possible Cultural Parallels

If black African vessels crossed the Atlantic, they carried an invisible cargo in addition to domesticated plants and utensils—those notions that would become tangibly expressed in the form of religious votive offerings, sculpture, painting and architecture. This invisible cargo was intellectual and linguistic; it could be lashed to no deck but was secure within the hearts and minds of the voyagers. Did this intangible intellectual cargo leave traces that influenced culture in the Americas?

I have always been suspicious of some of the evidence used to "prove" the theory of transoceanic cultural diffusion. To me, side-by-side photos of selected artworks of primitive peoples prove nothing for the simple reason that much primitive art is both crude and stylized in execution. Moreover, it is almost inevitable that somehow, somewhere, artistic representations of widely separated peoples can be found that are similar, if not identical, in appearance.

However, if presented in a conscientious way, as by Heyerdahl, such evidence may be persuasive: Heyerdahl took care to document similarities in specific artistic examples, generalized artistic motifs, the form of tools, linguistic similarities, blood-type relationships, and traditional histories of widely separated peoples in order to argue that contact must have occurred between them. Thus, Heyerdahl was able to show that on many levels the Polynesians of the Pacific islands were related both to Peruvians of about 500 A.D. and to later immigrants who arrived on the islands from the Northwest Coast of North America about 1200 A.D.

No such broad evidence can be presented to argue the case for black African contact with the Americas at an early time. Probably the most important reason for this impossibility is that the present picture has been considerably muddied by the fact that West Africans were imported, in great quantity, into the

Americas as slaves in post-Columbian times. Any evidence for pre-Columbian contact that might have been preserved in blood-group relationships and in linguistic relationships can be dismissed as resulting from later post-Columbian slave influence.

For instance, the great South American linguist, Jijón y Caamaño divides the Central American Chibchan languages into five groups. One of these groups is Mandinga, which is described merely as a "hybrid Negroid group" in the *Handbook of South American Indians* (page 177). This hybrid Negroid group of Chibchan is spoken in pockets from Nicaragua to the uplands of Colombia and Venezuela—exactly where we would expect, on other evidence, that black Africans penetrated along with their bottle gourds, plantains, cotton and metal-working in ancient pre-Columbian times.

Yet it is too easy to dismiss such linguistic evidence as later slave influence—too easy, and perhaps accurate. For many slaves did not meekly accept their fate. Some revolted against their masters immediately upon arriving in the New World and took to the bush to establish societies very similar to the African ones they had been taken from. This was as true in Belize, where such blacks were termed Black Caribs, as in Surinam, where they were and still are called Jukas. These people, until very recently, had no contact with the white social structure and lived in the bush far beyond the reach of official knowledge or authority. It is very possible that the African linguistic influence in the New World dates only from the fifteenth century A.D., but if it predates that, there is no way, now, to disentangle possible earlier influences in a way that will satisfy experts.

Yet it is at least suggestive that Jijón y Caamaño places the Chibchan group of languages among the Eastern Evolved Languages, which is to say among the oldest surviving languages of South America. This would argue that the "hybrid Negroid" component of Chibchan may predate slave importation. It is suggestive, but does not constitute proof.

Aside from the problems presented by the slave trade, there is an additional problem presented by the black Africans themselves. The Africans seem to have emphasized fusion and not conquest and domination when coming into contact with other groups, both in Africa and in the New World. If (as Davidson and Herskovits insist) the black African notion of proper "Earth Spirit enfranchisement" required them to adopt

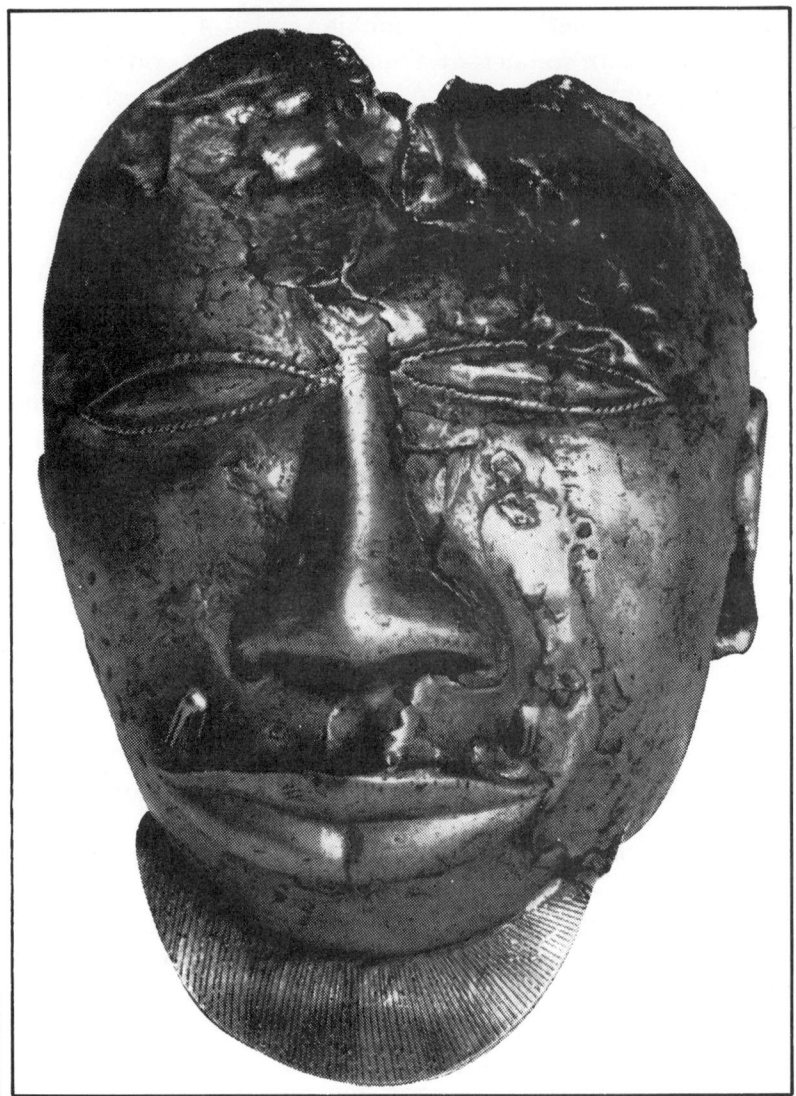

Basil Davidson

the gods and goddesses of the peoples and territories into which they migrated, how much more would black African visitors tend to adopt artistic styles, tool styles and lifestyles? If black African notions of proper "Earth Spirit enfranchisement" necessitated intermarriage with newly contacted people, how can such subtle contact ever be recognized after several thousand years have passed?

We would expect to see broad cultural similarities between West Africa and the New World only if black Africans had

The Akan death mask *from West Africa (left) is not particularly similar to the Muisca gold death mask from the upper Amazon basin (right), but the culture trait of making these gold death masks is common to West Africa and South America.*

arrived in the Americas in overwhelming numbers and had culturally absorbed the Amerindians instead of the other way around. Yet, in the epoch when contact seems most likely, about 1000 B.C., no people had succeeded in developing shipping capable of sustaining massive cultural contact across oceans. This became possible only in the fifteenth century A.D.

We may suspect that, given the area of apparent initial contact—the eastern Andean foothills of Venezuela and Colombia—this contact was important in the stimulation of American civilization since subsequent high cultures can seemingly be traced back to these eastern slopes where the great rivers begin to flow. But there is no proof that an "African" thread was central to the fabric of later American culture—or is there?

I think that a little careful and disciplined speculation can show that African culture contributed to some of the very basic religious and governmental concepts of later American civilizations and contributed, perhaps, very general ideas (not quite motifs) and "proper" pottery. The last contention is the least defensible and the most speculative, and I'll deal with it first.

Pottery Notions

One thing that is characteristic of much American pottery is the existence of multiple legs on bowls, pots and even on smaller cups. Strangely, these multiple legs are often bent outwards, like knees. Although some rare examples of this sort of pot-support can be found among almost all cultures producing ceramics, it is extremely common in the New World.

This sort of angular and multiple-leg pottery seems to betray a distant origin in a basically non-ceramic vessel-making tradition, as angular legs would logically develop in a culture using a working material of some strength.

Before it is fired, clay does not have much strength. Most real ceramic cultures have therefore adopted the practice of supporting their bowls, craters, cups and so forth on a single, central pedestal of considerable strength so that the clay of the object would not sag before being fired. This is, for instance, the Mediterranean tradition of pottery-making. Even when multiple legs were used in the Mediterranean fired pottery, they were generally straight—not bent at an angle.

There is one tradition of vessels supported with angular legs: that of the wooden bowls and cups of West Africa.

It seems to me that this style or idea of domestic vessels was taken to America, originally in the form of wooden utensils, and was later retained in American pottery as a distinctive feature. It certainly did not come from the Mediterranean tradition of ceramic design. A glance through any book on "primitive" art will show the basic similarity in idea existing between West African wooden-ware and American pottery of the angular multiple-leg type.

The Long Ears

When Pizarro first arrived in Inca territory, the ruling males were called "long ears" because they perforated and stretched the bottoms of their ear lobes. This stretching was accomplished by the insertion of heavy—usually gold—discs into the lobes. The existence of "long-eared" statues on Easter Island was one of Heyerdahl's pieces of evidence that the Pacific had been colonized by Peruvians.

There is also little doubt that, in addition to having long ears, the ruling Incas also possessed a fair bit of "Caucasoid" blood passed on to them by white gods of antiquity. Inca mummies reveal the existence of blond and red hair among past rulers and nobles—especially women. This Caucasoid admixture seems to have been more recent than the black contact. The whites seem to have come to Peru and begun their rule about 500 B.C. to 500 A.D. They must have been people from the Mediterranean, probably Phoenicians, Carthaginians or Celtiberians. No one knows.

But one thing we do know. Nowhere in the Mediterranean world and certainly not in the Mediterranean world of 500 B.C. to 500 A.D. will anyone find a tradition of "long ears" as a token of authority. Long ears seem to be characteristic only of the Incas and their Indian subjects and of the ancient West Africans. (If we find ear-lengthening now in Central Africa more than in West Africa in historic times, it is because, as Basil Davidson has explained, many of the Central African tribes originated in West Africa and migrated to their present homes within the last one or two thousand years.)

But ancient West Africans sculpture, and even recent sculpture depicting primordial people of the past, shows this long-eared characteristic.

It is possible that the first culture stimulated through black contact adopted the long-ear symbol of authority from the Africans. Subsequently, when later white invaders arrived from some as yet undisclosed source in the Mediterranean or North Africa, they adopted such local trappings of authority as ear lengthening so that their rule would be more readily accepted. They then imposed their own ideas of sun-king worship, with themselves as rulers.

It is difficult, if not impossible, without accepting both black and white influence in formative concepts of organization, to

Long Ears
Peruvian gold figurines (above) and modern West African wood carving of ancient ("primordial") couple (right). The man is on the right in each pair.

imagine how one could find partly Caucasoid rulers of an Amerindian nation adopting the trappings of authority otherwise known only from ancient tropical Africa.

Quetzalcoatl/Kukulcan (The Feathered Serpent)

From the zoological point of view, the notion of a feathered serpent presents no problems in terms of the latest evolutionary theory. Birds' feathers are, after all, no more than highly evolved reptilian scales. The notion of a feathered serpent might even be enjoyable to a paleontologist. But it does puzzle both zoologists and ethnologists concerned with events that occurred more recently than 60 million years ago. How did the

idea of a feathered serpent come about? Why, once conceived, was the feathered serpent connected to rain-making of all things? What kind of snake did the ancient Mexicans know that was both large, and for some reason, could be compared with a tropical bird of colorful plumage? Finally, why make this feathered serpent into a major deity?

I think that all of these questions can be answered, but only in relation to zoology—and specifically African zoology. The conceptual links will become clear.

The first thing to be dealt with is the matter of large snakes. The most common large snake of Mexico is the rattlesnake, which can reach a length of eight feet. Huge rattlesnakes are portrayed in Mayan art, notably at Chichen Itza; they are sculpted about twice the snake's maximum length and much more than maximum thickness. But Quetzalcoatl is really huge. The feathered serpent may stretch, in undulation, the

Basil Davidson

Carved relief on Kushite temple *at Naga, Sudan, showing that the motif of a giant serpent is also African. The python was an African symbol of wisdom. In drier areas of Africa, such as Egypt, where there are no pythons, the symbolism was transferred to the cobra.*

entire length of a building's facade. Assuming that the ancient Mexicans were interested in keeping some sense of proportion and did not simply make Quetzalcoatl/Kukulcan huge because he was of supreme importance, we may assume that the feathered serpent was known to be several times the length of a rattlesnake. This leaves us with a question: why would anyone conceptualize a snake much larger than any known to exist? Or, did the ancient Mexicans know of snakes two or three times as long as the biggest rattlesnake?

The largest known American snake is the anaconda (*Eunectes murinus*). Experts disagree on the size it can reach. North American armchair experts allow nineteen to twenty feet, but embattled Brazilian experts on the spot are strangely quiet on

Mexican carving of the feathered serpent Quetzalcoatl. *Jade mosaic on stone.*

the subject. The institute at Butantan in Brazil has an anaconda skin thirty-three feet long, and while a certain amount of stretching is usual when a snake is skinned, the hide must have come from a twenty-six-foot-long living serpent.[1]

Anacondas, per se, are restricted to the Amazon basin and do not range as far north as Mexico. Perhaps the ancient Mexicans had heard of anacondas and fashioned their feathered serpent along anaconda dimensions. This might even seem likely if, as I have suggested, the beginning of Mexican civilization came out of the eastern Andean slopes where anacondas certainly dwell in the headwaters of the Orinoco, Amazon and Rio Negro.

But the anaconda makes a poor Quetzalcoatl. The feathered serpent was linked to the quetzal bird, which boasts resplendent plumage. The anaconda is a colorless snake with a dirty white stomach and a rather dismal olive-colored upper surface relieved only by a monotonous pattern of equally dreary chocolate-colored oval rings or spots. Besides, anacondas are very rarely seen, as they spend most of their time under muddy water, presumably waiting for things like capybaras to come within their ken. A more unlikely source for Quetzalcoatl can hardly be imagined. Anacondas have nothing particularly colorful, regal or smart about them. They are altogether humdrum, feeding upon large rodents and otherwise pretty torpid. There are few reliable accounts of anacondas partaking of a repast so dramatic as a man, although several horses have been devoured. In combing the legends, myth and folklore of the Amazonian Indians, I have been unable to find much interest in the anaconda. These people rightly fear the electric eel, the *didi* (apparently an unknown ape) and the jaguar much more than the anaconda.

The same things cannot be said of Old World pythons. Pythons come in anaconda sizes:

> A French traveler, Charles Mayer, brought back alive to Europe a reticulated python from Asia which was 32 feet long. Another naturalist, William Hornaday, killed a 30-foot python (in Africa). These are the largest specimens which are known with certainty.[2]

Moreover, the Old World pythons are strikingly marked. In fact, the plastic imitation snakeskin making a comeback in disco circles is more or less imitation python skin brightly colored in patterns of green, blue and red. Moreover, African culture has consistently chosen the snake—either python or cobra, depending upon availability—as the symbol of wisdom and spiritual development. The Temple of the Sun in Naga in the old black empire of Kush is adorned with pythons wriggling skyward, and this artistic motif bears the most striking resemblance to Aztec and Mayan representations of the feathered serpent.

Old World pythons are the only huge snakes that can reasonably be associated with something as colorful as a quetzal bird, but they can also reasonably be equated with the sun and with rain.

This is, again, speculative. But not purely speculative because we will see that precisely the same conceptual links have been made by a people who doubtless never had any contact with either the black Africans or the ancient Mexicans, the Australian aborigines:

> According to the Australian blackfellows, some of these legendary creatures still exist . . . the rainbow snake, called *mindi* on the lower Murray River . . . has a large head, and when it hisses its tongue is seen to have three points. When it slides over the top of a tree, hanging onto the branches with its prehensile tail, it looks just like a rainbow. . . . The legendary *mindi* is no doubt based on a distorted picture of the diamond python, found only in the coastal region . . . its body is covered with spots in almost all the colors of the rainbow—which phenomenon, by the way, must be extremely rare in a continent where the rainfall is less than 20 inches a year.[3]

The same can be said of Old World pythons of Africa—they are rainbow marked, which links them both to the shining sun and to rainfall; they are arboreal (unlike the aquatic anaconda); and some of their markings resemble feathers on a bird. Such a creature would be a good symbol of wisdom or spiritual development as it would often be seen in the tops of trees, obviously attempting to move as close as possible to the source of life and energy, the sun.

At the same time, the python has the good sense to live in deep burrows in the earth—by night—and therefore it realizes the connection between the sun above and the earth below, honoring equally the female principles of earth and moon and the male principles of air and sun. Furthermore, any creature who imitates the rain-proved colors of the rainbow, and knows how to bring life-giving rain in such places as the Upper Nile and Australia, not to mention Mexico, must assuredly be wise.

The Nauer people of the Upper Nile today, no less than the ancient Kushites of old, invest the python with all sort of awesome and spiritual attributes. Pythons probably became extinct on the Lower Nile before the Egyptians settled there, and the Egyptians transferred the python's attributes to the largest snake they knew—the cobra. It, too, lives in burrows by night, but may dance to the sun during the day, especially if confronted with a man, another sentient creature who recognizes the balance of life existing between earth and sun. Similarly, the Bantu, when they migrated onto the veldt of Southern

Africa, transferred the spiritual attributes to the yellow cobra as soon as they left the python-country of the great lakes.

I think that the characteristics of Quetzalcoatl have been sufficiently traced back to black African origins, since there were no pythons to inspire ancient Egyptians or other men of the Mediterranean coastal regions in historic times. However, there is an artistic motif that, I believe, clinches the matter. Quetzalcoatl is often depicted as a serpent of huge dimensions with a man's face often shown within the snake's mouth.

The Mexicans knew of no snake that could reasonably be imagined to devour a man. The anaconda far to the south may have devoured men on rare occasions, but it seems inclined toward capybaras. The Old World pythons, both in Africa and in Asia, however are a real, though doubtless a greatly exaggerated, danger to people. The pythons' arboreal habits result in their dropping onto people making their way down jungle paths, especially en route to washing and watering places. The surprise and fear of the humans on such occasions instinctively leads to struggle, to which the python responds, often with tragic results. This danger of pythons, whether realistic or not, was sufficiently important psychologically that both American and French adventurers in Southeast Asia were given anti-python hand-to-hand combat lessons.

Whether justified or not, I cannot shake off the feeling that Mexican representations of a man peeking out from Quetzalcoatl's mouth—along with the colors, scale-color patterns, sun-seeking and earth-burrowing habits, and rainbow associations—reflect traditions about Old World pythons, but these associations, in Old World historical times, could only have been brought to the Mexicans by black Africans since these attributes had either been transferred to the cobra, or forgotten entirely, by men of the Mediterranean in about 1000 B.C. and later.

To speculate further, the wisdom attributes attached to pythons may have come also from its occasional attempts to devour, or at least attack, men—the other sentient creature in the python's domain. We know that the roots of cannibalism are not merely the lust for human flesh as food, but the attempt to ingest the qualities of those eaten. A similar desire may well have been attributed to the python who, wise itself, might want to increase its wisdom by the occasional ingestion of another sun-and-earth worshiping creature, man. It is more than possible that this primal association was made in the lost Saharan world. Bones of the now-extinct Gigantophis, a python about sixty feet long, have been found in the drier parts of Egypt. In pre-historical times, the Gigantophis may well have existed in the Sahara, giving rise to snake worship in a manner impossible to forget.

At all events, one must explain Quetzalcoatl in terms of human faces peeking from within a snake's mouth. Such explanations are hard to come by without recourse to African zoology.

The idea and godhead of Quetzalcoatl seems to be a conceptual complex that has many components familiar to us in the myth and belief structures of the Old World. At the same time, the zoological aspects of Quetzalcoatl seem also to be based upon Old World fauna to a great degree. It is probable that the idea of Quetzalcoatl resulted from a fusion of conceptions. The ancient Mexicans may have originally worshiped the quetzal bird in some manner or other, probably as a minor deity. Then foreigners came with their snake-worship, which was linked to sun-and-earth worship and grafted this onto the indigenous quetzal belief-structure. This fusion would be natural in that the python of the newcomers and the quetzal bird of the local inhabitants shared coloration. Depending on the species of python, the skin-pattern may have been reminiscent of the overlay of bird's feathers.

If this analysis has any claim to validity, it is an easy matter to eliminate white candidates for the "foreign" components of Quetzalcoatl. Since the Yucatan culture complex seems to have begun during the first few centuries B.C., we can say for certain that no people of the Mediterranean brought the serpent part of Quetzalcoatl; for surely they would have brought the Egyptian cobra and not what is obviously a python. Pythons were extinct around the Mediterranean by 500 B.C.

This sort of symbolism can only have been brought from tropical Africa. We may remember that at about this time Kush was falling back from Egypt under the iron blows of Assyria and, later, Persia. We have been told that "the sons of Kush, very numerous, marched toward the setting sun." Doubtless, they carried with them their religious ideas, including the python-sun-earth-rain complex that seems to be represented on the temple at Naga. We would seem to have the plausible serpent component for Quetzalcoatl in the beliefs of Kush about 600 to 300 B.C., which is when the Yucatan culture complex seems to have begun in the form similar to that which the Spanish found.

I think that we are justified in speculating that Quetzalcoatl was an idea resulting from a fusion of native Amerindian conceptions and imported Kushite ones. The feathered serpent can be ascribed to a specific migration of people at a specific time.

For although characteristic of Meso-America, the idea of Quetzalcoatl is only vaguely represented in South American belief structures. As such, I think it is related to the specific Kushite migration rather than to the very first unknown black visitors who arrived in the Amazonian headwaters 500 to 1,000 years earlier and who brought their bottle gourds, plantains, cotton and precious metal-working knowledge to the New World. The culture that existed in Yucatan when the probable Kushites came ashore possibly owed much to the beginnings of civilization in South America, but the two distinct black contacts were essentially separate and unconnected.

It is interesting to examine the clothing of those black warriors in the temple murals of Chichen Itza. They wear an Egyptian-like kilt, as do the Amerindian warriors shown in the same murals. This compares well with the kilt worn on Kushite reliefs depicting the lion god. It is possible, therefore, that Meso-American clothing was influenced greatly by the same black migration that brought the notion of Quetzalcoatl.

Again, just as with the long-eared token of authority in Peru, the idea of Quetzalcoatl was used and modified by white visitors of a later date. First, there was a bearded old white man, very kind, who was likened to Quetzalcoatl, probably because of his wisdom: this is the legendary human Quetzalcoatl. Then, some time later, from about 900 to 1000 A.D., there was a white king of the Toltecs, the fifth Toltec king, and he conquered the New Empire of the Mayas and subsequently adopted the idea of Quetzalcoatl as a sort of kingly title, doubtless in order to legitimize his rule as other whites in Peru seem to have adopted the local long-ear token of authority.

These various Quetzalcoatls should not be confused. First, there was the idea and godhead of Quetzalcoatl. Second, there was a specific old and bearded man who was likened to Quetzalcoatl, apparently because of his wisdom. Third, there was a white ruler who appropriated the mystique of Quetzalcoatl as a governmental technique. In addition to these two white men, there were other contacts with whites that had nothing to do with Quetzalcoatl; one of these is shown in the murals in the Temple of Warriors.

In conclusion, the black contacts were not without their significance. Certain basic ideas of authority and belief appear to have come from a very ancient fusion of black African and Amerindian concepts. This old and fundamental cultural fusion seems to have the conceptual basis for American proto-civilization both in South America and in Central America and, from this beginning, distinctive civilizations evolved in the New World, incorporating later and essentially independent cultural infusions from the Old World.

10
White Gods and Lost Cities

Almost everyone has the vague idea that somehow and sometime white men came to the Americas before Columbus. This theme has been the subject of any number of popular books like Pierre Honoré's *In Search of the White Gods* and even hovers behind the academic arguments of scholarly works like Heyerdahl's *American Indians in the Pacific*.

The simple explanation for our fascination with pre-Columbian voyages to America is curiosity. There is evidence that Europeans did get to the New World before Columbus, yet we do not know exactly who the first explorers were. Were they Ancient Egyptians, Carthagenians, Irish priests, Norsemen? The identity of these visitors remains a mystery, and mysteries are fascinating.

Maybe there is another reason for a preoccupation with white men in the Americas before Columbus. An ethnocentric reason: if the white men came, and if they are remembered in some legends as white gods, then can Europeans not take credit for the development of civilization in the New World? Our racial vanity is flattered by this possibility; we are not obligated to extend the capability of civilization to the American Indians. Unfortunately for our self-conceptions, however, the evidence argues another way. There is not much doubt that white men came to the New World before Columbus, and they must have had some influence. They were remembered in some legends. But they did not have a great deal of cultural influence, and they certainly did not begin American civilizations in the Mediterranean mold—otherwise there would be much more similarity between Old and New World civilizations. We would not have the problem of chronology that puzzles diffusionist archeologists.

But perhaps there is a third reason why both popular and academic histories are often preoccupied with pre-Columbian voyages to the New World. This third reason involves the inexplicable facts surrounding the Conquest of the Aztecs and Incas.

The truth is not only sometimes stranger than fiction, it is sometimes so much more unlikely that, if we did not know it to be the truth, only purveyors of the most imaginative fantasy would consent to publish it. The Conquest of the New World was not merely bizarre; by any standards, it was an utterly fantastic event. Just the statistics are strange: 553 Spaniards under Hernando Cortés defeated the Aztec Empire with a handful of cannon and a few horses; 170 Spaniards under Francisco Pizarro, with fewer cannon and fewer horses, ended the Inca Empire. Even if the Indians lacked firearms, and were justly terrified of the horses, these facts alone cannot and do not explain the Spanish victories.

Both Aztecs and Incas boasted disciplined armies numbering in the tens of thousands of men, their societies were highly evolved and they were in some ways more civilized than their European opponents. It is reasonable to imagine that under normal circumstances their fear of guns and horses would gradually have worn off and they would have overwhelmed the Spaniards with sheer numbers and courage. For these soldiers of Aztec and Inca lands were not afraid of death, as their conduct in their own wars testified. Death by horse or gun, after the initial terror of the unexpected had been accepted, could be no worse than death by club, arrow or javelin. Certainly, it would be preferable to being a live sacrifice and having one's beating heart torn from one's chest through an opening slowly cut with a flint knife. Yet there are captives of Aztec record who chose sacrificial death over an honorable post in the Aztec army, because being a sacrifice would bring the reward of warriors' heaven. Such men are unlikely to have remained terrified by horses and guns for long.

Logically then, we are entitled to expect that the Spanish would have won a few initial easy victories, but then suffer massacres; the business of the Conquest should have been a protracted war of the most brutal sort. The Spanish advantage in fire-power should have been outweighed by the enormous numbers of Indian warriors. The Spanish were a long way from home by slow caravel and could have built up their number only slowly.

The Spaniards might never have achieved total conquest, but

circumstances during the Conquest were anything but normal. They were fantastic. And the fantasy was enacted, almost identically, in both Mexico and Peru. As Paul Herrmann has aptly put it, "the Spanish were doubly dumbfounded"[1] by what actually happened. The more intelligent Americanists have been equally perplexed ever since.

In the spring of 1519 Cortés and his little fleet came to anchor in the estuary of the Tabasco River. Very shortly thereafter they met the local Indians in a battle that the Spaniards' ten brass cannons and four culverins turned into a rout. Terrified and defeated, the local ruler, the Cacique of Cintla, sent gifts in an effort to appease Cortés: twenty beautiful young maidens bedecked with gold, and an undisclosed number of their slaves also wearing gold ornaments. One of these girls was called, in Aztec, Malintzin; she was an Aztec princess who had been exiled by Montezuma. Malintzin was light skinned and haughty; but upon seeing Cortés she went up to him, looked closely, and fell back to the deck of the ship on her knees. Cortés was not a little astonished; but, assisted by half-trained *indios* interpreters from Spanish-held islands in the Caribbean, he was gradually enlightened by the following story told by Malintzin:

> Once, long ago, other white men came to Mexico in long ships that looked like serpents crawling over the sea. These men wore serpent ornaments on their helmets. They must be representatives of the sacred serpent, Quetzalcoatl. The strangers settled in Yucatan, among the Mayas, and some say that one of these white men ruled over the Mayas. But at length the Mayas revolted against him and he fled eastward, where he embarked on a ship to return across the sea whence he had come. But before he left he foretold that someday his white brothers beyond the sunrise would come to Mexico and conquer it.

It was clear to this Aztec lady that Cortés and his men must be the returning brothers of the whites who had come long before. They must be the white gods of legend.

The scene just painted is somewhat imaginary. None of Cortés' biographers knew, or recorded if they did, what took place on the night that Cortés met his lovely mistress, "the only woman he really loved throughout his turbulent life."[2] For Malintzin became Cortés' Doña Marina, his only trustworthy companion. But it is likely that Malintzin would have related this Mayan story to Cortés. It is likelier still that she would have related a similar tradition current in the "halls of Montezuma" that was just then greatly troubling that unhappy monarch. After all, Malintzin could have no great love for the Aztec emperor, having been sold by him to the Mayas as a slave.

And the fact is that Montezuma and the Aztecs were alarmed by portents that seemed to indicate some pending judgment of the gods. Comets appeared in the sky, the lake of Texcoco overflowed its banks, augurs predicted gloomy things from the flights of birds. All this had been going on for some time before Cortés had even heard of Mexico. Aztec poets lamented:

> How sad! How heavy!
> I know that our kingdom is sinking,
> The stars are smoking,
> The city of books, of flowers
> Will soon be no more!³

The problem was that the year I Reed was approaching. This year recurs every fifty-two years in the Aztec calendar. It was the year when the white gods had come in legend, and therefore the year when they might reasonably be expected to return. One of the earliest chroniclers of the Conquest, Aztec Prince Ixtlilxochitl, tells us that Montezuma, upon being crowned emperor, was given the traditional warning that the rule of Mexico was not his, but held in stewardship for the white gods.

By one of the most incredible coincidences of history, Cortés had landed and had fought the battle that brought him Doña Marina on the Aztec date 9 wind, I Reed, which was exactly the date worked out by Aztec priests as to the most probable arrival of the white gods—Maundy Thursday, April 22, 1519, in our reckoning.

Thus, it is no wonder that Emperor Montezuma and the Aztecs were depressed. They were psychologically beaten before they started. And that is how 500-odd Spaniards could walk from the Tabasco estuary to Mexico City through country controlled by the Aztecs. True, the horses and the guns terrified, and Cortés rallied disgruntled Aztec vassals; but the real explanation is that Montezuma knew it was the end. Had he offered whole-hearted resistance from the beginning, there is no doubt that the Aztecs could have crushed the tiny Spanish force.

Legends of white gods varied a bit even within specific localities. The Spaniard Juan de Torquemada writes on the subject of Quetzalcoatl:

> A few years after the settlement of Tollan, certain tribes came from northern regions and landed in the area of Panuco. These were well-dressed people who wore long garments of black sacking, similar to those worn by the Turks, etc. and resembling the *soutanes* of priests; these garments were open in front, without cowls, cut out around the neck, and with short, wide sleeves that did not reach as far as the elbows. The natives still wear them today during their dances when they wish to represent those tribes. The latter pushed on indefatigably from Panuco without encountering any hostility, and when in due course of time they came to Tollan they were very friendly received there, for they were very experienced and skilled and of great inventiveness and artistry. They understood the working of gold and silver and were masters of every art, e.g., they were excellent lapidaries; they showed the greatest dexterity not only in such fine things as these, however, but also in other activities of a more utilitarian nature and in agriculture. In short, their admirable behavior, industry and skill made them so well liked that wherever they went they were highly esteemed and shown great honor.... When the newcomers saw that they could not find a livelihood in Tollan, since the country was already densely populated, they sought to move on again and settled in Cholula, where they were also very friendly received; and the natives of the district, as is well-known, intermarried with them. For a long time they settled there and took root. The following story is told in this locality: When those tribes arrived in Tollan, they had with them a very distinguished person who was their leader and ruled over them. His name was Quetzalcoatl; the people of Cholula revered him as a god. It is generally agreed that he was of pleasant exterior: white, fair-haired, bearded, finely built....
>
> It is asserted that Quetzalcoatl lived for twenty years in Cholula, and that at the end of this period he returned by the same route on which he had come. When he left he took with him four distinguished and virtuous youths from that city, but sent them back from Coatbacoalco, enjoining them

to observe the good precepts which he had given them and to make the following announcement to the inhabitants of the City of Cholula: Let them rest assured that at some future time white men with long beards like himself would come across the sea from the east. These men, his brothers, would become lords of the land of Mexico. Therefore the Indians always awaited the fulfilment of this prophecy, and when they saw the Christians arrive they called them gods, sons and brothers of Quetzalcoatl; although when they got to know and experience their works, they could by no means continue to regard them as divine.[4]

This story does not sound exactly the same as the Mayan "Wotan" legend that I have put into the mouth of Doña Marina, but there are some curious parallels. It is known that a king of Tula (Tollan) did go into Maya land, occupy Chichen Itza, and apparently style himself "Quetzalcoatl." However, it would seem that the "snake-people in snake-ships" of the Mayas cannot have been the Quetzalcoatl of Juan de Torquemada's narrative.

Walter Krickeberg has cautioned against accepting the white god legends as recorded and reported by early chroniclers at face value and as sober history. Krickeberg's opinion—and it is one of much weight, still—is that while all these legends may have a kernel of historical fact to them they have been heavily encrusted with post-Conquest Christian embellishments. Therefore, we should not necessarily bother to sort out one Quetzalcoatl from another as historical personages. We should take the entire legend cycle to mean merely that there was some pre-Columbian white contact of some sort at some time in the distant past:

> All other elements in the American legends which offer striking parallels to early Christian stories are merely to be counted amongst the great number of correspondences between the civilized peoples of the Old World and the New, which also exist in other spheres and whose explanation must be left to future research.[5]

That may be, but it is very tempting to relate the Mayan Wotan legend to some errant Norse expedition, and to relate the obviously monkish Quetzalcoatl of Juan de Torquemada's story with some equally well-traveled Christian priest. This is not to say that they are mutually exclusive since, after about 1000 A.D., the Norse themselves adopted Christianity, much to Eric the Red's chagrin. It was about the year 1000 A.D. or a little later that the Quetzalcoatl of Tollan did, indeed, invade Yucatan and install himself as ruler of Chichen Itza, so there is a possible correspondence between the Mayan and the Toltec versions.

We can follow the white god legends from Mexico right down through Central America into Colombia, on to Peru, and even out into the Pacific.

The Chibcha-speaking peoples insist that a bearded old man of great virtue came to them in the past. His name was Bochica. Bochica spoke with their king, Nompanem, and told him of what he had to teach. Nompanem saw that Bochica's teachings were good and commanded that they should be followed throughout the land.

> And Nompanem asked Bochica: "What punishment is meet for him that doth not obey thy teaching?"
> Said Bochica: "Thou shalt not compel obedience to my teaching with the punishments of this world. Beyond, in the other world, there are punishments for the evil and rewards for those who obey the teachings of God."[6]

In addition to this Christian-like spiritual fare, Bochica brought also knowledge of agriculture, astronomy, weaving and civil organization.

Much the same story was cherished by the Peruvians in Inca times, but overlaid with the "rightful God-rulers will return" theme that so tormented Montezuma in Mexico.

The chronicler Pedro de Candia was Cretan by birth, but had been knighted by the King of Spain; he was with Pizarro's successful expedition against the Incas. He relates that the Spanish were astounded that the inhabitants of Tumbez, the first Peruvian town they entered, fell flat on their faces in the presence of the Spaniards and said, "Viracocha," with great reverence. Linguistic study seems to have ascertained that *viracocha* means, literally, "sea-foam" or maybe "sea-grease." In any case it is a reference to oceanic white caps, and is applied to white men in honor of a white man who came from the sea in former times and who left by sea into the Pacific. Later usage of the word emphasized the godlike character of this visitor, who taught that there was a power higher than the sun, and *viracocha* came to mean something like "sun of the sun." It means simply "lord" among native Peruvians, Bolivians and some people of Ecuador and is—or was before Marxist dialectics made considerable inroads—applied with respect to white men. In the course of time Viracocha either became or was confused with another Peruvian deity, Illa Tiki or Kon Tiki, a god of thunder and lightning. Eventually a phrase like "Kon Tiki Viracocha" could be used to mean a reverence for the most powerful power, a creator god.

The basic story is clear enough. When the Incas came into power in Peru, Viracocha had long been known. It was said that Viracocha and his white followers had built the city of Tiahuanaco on the shores of Lake Titicaca in Bolivia. They had also built the holy city of Pachacamac in Peru south of Lima, and had founded the city of Cuzco, which the Incas appropriated as their own capital and administrative center. They were well respected. Viracocha carried a cross and wept for the sins of the world; he baptized some of the people. But Viracocha and his fellows were attacked by King Cari of the Coquimbotal tribe, and most of the white men were slain, although the lives of their women and children were spared. Viracocha led these survivors and with a few loyal native followers down to the Pacific coast. There, Viracocha preached a farewell sermon with the usual theme that his brothers would someday come and rule the Peruvians. Then "he spread his cloak upon the sea, stood upon it with his followers, and departed," which Heyerdahl understands to mean that Viracocha and his people departed upon balsa rafts.[9]

It is an astonishing circumstance, the significance of which Heyerdahl was the first to realize. The Polynesians count their origin from the god Kon Tiki who came across the sea from the east, the South American mainland. (The Peruvian and Polynesian legends therefore dovetail, and this, together with material cultural parallels, convinced Heyerdahl to undertake the famous *Kon Tiki* voyage in order to prove that Polynesia could have been peopled from the east. All the experts had had them coming from the other direction.)

The situation is somewhat complicated by the fact that the seventh Inca, Hatun Tupac, who began his rule about 1350, adopted the name of Viracocha because of unusual and dramatic events. His father, the sixth Inca, named Yahuar Huaccac, was the only incompetent Inca ruler and proved indecisive when confronted with an invasion threat posed by the Chanca people. The Chanca people moved on Cuzco itself, but still the cowardly Yahuar Huaccac made no move to stop them. At this point, Prince Hatun Tupac had a dream in which the white and bearded figure of Viracocha appeared to him and gave counsel as to how the Chancas might be stopped. Accordingly, Prince Hatun Tupac gathered together a sort of private army and narrowly defeated the Chancas. Upon becoming the seventh Inca ruler he apparently adopted the name of his dream-mentor, Viracocha. Hutan Tupac (Viracocha Inca) ruled until about 1400 A.D. and was, perhaps, the greatest Peruvian monarch of all.

But this Inca ruler should not be confused with the Viracocha who was revered long before the Incas came to power in Peru. If Polynesian legends can be relied upon and if we can assume that the original Viracocha really did begin Polynesian history with his desperate Pacific voyage, then there is a possibility of dating the departure of this bearded white leader.

Archeology on Pacific Islands has established that the first wave of colonists arrived from South America about 500 A.D. These first immigrants built in stone on Easter Island and other places; they were "long-ears." About 1200 A.D., other people began arriving on the islands from the Northwest Coast of North America. At first these newcomers were content to be ruled by the long-eared sons of Kon Tiki, but eventually—on Easter Island at least—there was a general revolt against long-eared rule about 1400 A.D. The newcomers refused to help the long-ears erect any more giant statues, and began to tear statues down. At some point the long-ears retreated to a point of the island and dug a defensive trench across the spit. In a great battle, all the long-ears were slain, except one who was allowed to live as a representative of his people. Thus did the story of Viracocha's people end, and not so very long before the Spanish and Dutch "discovered" the islands.[7]

If Viracocha and his followers built Tiahuanaco and several other cities and had time to migrate from Lake Titicaca into Peru, there were obviously several generations of Viracochas and white followers before the advent of the Viracocha who took his rafts into the Pacific. The chronology of Viracocha tallies, more or less, with the accepted dates for the Tiahuanaco culture, which is supposed to have flourished in the first centuries A.D. Viracocha and his followers were obviously early Christians, and could be ascribed to any number of times and places.

Two major points immediately spring to mind with respect to these various white gods: First, these legends do not refer to the same person or group of people or the same times. The Quetzalcoatl of Mexico cannot be the bearded old man of Colombia and of Peru. It is too much to expect that one man, already old and bearded upon his arrival in Tollan, could spend twenty years in Cholula, leave Mexico, spend more years teaching in Colombia as Bochica and still have time remaining to continue his good work in Peru, before carrying his missionary work to the Pacific. We are obviously faced with successive missionaries, some of whom came with followers (Viracocha, Quetzalcoatl) and some of whom apparently came alone (Bochica). Then, there is a class of white gods who do not appear to be "Christian-like" at all. In this class is the Quetzalcoatl/Kukulcan who set himself up in Chichen Itza and who apparently either began or emphasized the practice of throwing maidens into the *cenote*. The "snake-people" of the Wotan legends do not sound like kindly Quetzalcoatls/Bochicas and Viracochas, and the naked white warriors of the Temple of Warriors murals are certainly not in this category. In fact, we see several visitations by whites.

But the second consideration is most important. It is obvious from the context of the legends themselves that although these whites often managed to rule for a period of time, they also almost inevitably came into conflict with the indigenous norms and values. They may have been admired for their arts and sciences, but they were sooner or later deposed or otherwise revolted against. Also, the legends make it quite clear that there was a relatively high culture when these whites came because, although they were often acknowledged to be masters of various arts, the arts themselves were known and practiced by people already inhabiting a given area. Only Bochica is said to have brought entirely new knowledge; but his legend comes from a people who did not possess the level of culture of those in Mexico or Peru. Even so, there was enough social organization for the teachings of Bochica to be instituted throughout the realm of Nompanem and enough cultural base for the teachings in agriculture, astronomy, etc. to be adopted. Even these Colombians could not have been untutored savages.

We are forced to the conclusion that the white gods did not really influence the culture in a basic way, even though they were long remembered by the people who, in the end, usually rejected them. The only basic and extremely significant way in which these white gods affected American civilization was in the manner Cortés experienced. The legends provided a foundation for acceptance of future white rulers that sapped the Amerindian civilizations' will to resist.

The incredible coincidence of Cortés and the Aztecs was repeated with Pizarro and the Incas. There had been a tradition, perhaps a prophecy of Viracocha himself, that after the time of twelve Incas had passed, other people would come to rule Peru. Astoundingly, Atahualpa, the thirteenth Inca, had hardly achieved undisputed power when news of Pizarro's landing was brought to him.

The twelfth Inca ruler, Huayna Capac, declared upon his deathbed:

> Many years ago it was revealed to me by our father, the Sun, that after the rule of twelve of his children, an alien people would come which had never been seen before in these regions and would conquer and subdue this kingdom and many others as well. I am inclined to suppose that this refers to the people recently sighted off our shores. They are said to be a powerful race, superior to us in everything. Now we know that with me the number of twelve Incas has been reached. Therefore I predict to you that a few years after I have gone to my ancestors, that strong people will appear and bring to fulfilment the prophecy of my father, the Sun; they will conquer our kingdom and rule over us. I command you to obey and serve them.[8]

What with Cortés landing in the year I Reed and Pizarro appearing in the time of the thirteenth Inca it is hardly surprising that these empires were overwhelmed. The most ancient prophecies were fulfilled. It is rather like the Russians perfecting a method of projecting holographic illusions in the atmosphere so that, one fine day, the Western world of "Christendom" suddenly woke up to the apparition of childhood visions of God and the Heavenly Host suspended in mid-air while a deep voice boomed, "It's Armageddon time!" However cynical our own epoch, there is no doubt that such an occurrence would spread both deserved panic and righteous fervor among much of the population. The resulting chaos might make us easy victims for more conventional methods of military aggression.

The circumstances of the Conquest are so fantastic that I think anyone might be forgiven considering a supernatural aspect to it. The whole business was, at the very least, most mysterious. And this is undoubtedly why only a very small number of Americanists and historians have paid attention to these legends at all. It has proved more convenient for some of them to create another modern scientific myth by asserting that these legends are themselves myths, that they were made up by the Spanish as a propaganda weapon to assist in the process of the Conquest. Paul Herrmann has shown that although the white god legends did manifestly contribute to the Conquest (and it would therefore be convenient to dismiss the difficulties they present by attributing them to post-Columbian propaganda machinations of the Spanish), they are pre-Columbian and could not have been manufactured by the likes of Cortés and Pizarro. Aztec pictographs dating from before 1492 show some of the ill-omens that so depressed the soldiers and courtiers of Montezuma. Second, in Peru, the Incas or some Peruvians before them had constructed a statue of their Viracocha; it undeniably portrayed a white man. The Spaniards themselves mistook this statue of Viracocha for a statue of St. Bartholomew.

Moreover, as Herrmann points out, if the Spaniards had concocted these white god legends, surely they would have drawn the native picture of the white gods in a manner more in keeping with their own Mediterranean appearance. Very few Spaniards approximated the traditional description of Quetzalcoatl or Viracocha. The Spaniards of the time, as today, were dark haired and olive complexioned for the most part. Indeed, some of the ruling Incas who boasted some Viracocha blood were lighter skinned than the Spaniards. Pedro Pizarro, Francisco's cousin, wrote. "These people are corn-blond. . . . Some of the ladies and gentlemen were actually whiter than Spaniards. I saw one woman with her child here of a whiteness such as is seldom seen. The Indians believe such people to be children of the *idolos*, the gods."[9]

Peruvian mummies recovered by modern archeologists support the truth of Pizarro's statement, though it had been dismissed as a fable by "the older generation of Americanists, who laid particular stress on the Mongolian features of the Indians."[10] Some Andean mummies undeniably show blond and even red hair of typical Caucasoid waviness. (Color photographs of these locks can be seen in Thor Heyerdahl's *American Indians in the Pacific.*)

It is clear, then, that not only did the majority of Spaniards not match up to the white gods' whiteness—which, in fact, caused some Indians to doubt the Spanish relationship to them in spite of the prophecies and the coincidences—but there is undeniable literary, statuary and physiological material proving conclusively that the American Indians had been introduced to pre-Columbian white people. The mummies themselves show that the Indians' legends were correct to the degree that some of these white gods had entered the local ruling classes, for only important people were mummified at all.

Thus, the white gods and the coincidences concerning the uncannily opportune arrival of the Spanish constitute a real mystery whose solution will not be discovered by the fashionable modern method of pretending that no mystery exists and by attributing the legends to modern propaganda procedures.

Another mystery has similarly been dismissed by modern experts with the simple assertion that "it doesn't exist." Maybe it should be "they don't exist," because the mystery concerns any number of lost cities alleged to be located in the Amazon Basin. Perhaps the Spaniards were the first to hear of these cities which, naturally, were supposed to contain vast quantities of gold. The idea of El Dorado was eventually applied to such a lost city or land of lost cities, although originally it seems to have been attached to a historical personage. (See Chapter Five.)

The modern cycle of lost city stories undoubtedly began with Major Percy Fawcett:

> In 1906 the race for rubber was on, and to get it dirt cheap settlers did not shrink from enslaving the Amazon Indians, flogging, torturing and even killing them at the slightest whim. The tribes that resisted were massacred, their villages pillaged and burnt. Officials and soldiers sent to keep order were as savage and cruel as the *seringueiros.* In the rich rubber plantations along the Rio Abuna and the River Acre (Rio Macarinarra), which marks the southern boundary of

Brazil, the northern frontier of Bolivia and part of that of Peru, a bitter dispute arose between the three countries about the exact position of their frontiers. War was on the point of breaking out.

The Royal Geographical Society of London was called in to act as mediator and sent Major Percy Fawcett, an artillery officer of 39, to make a thorough survey of the area in dispute. It was to perform this thankless task that he first penetrated the vast forests of the Amazon, in which he vanished without a trace 20 years later.[11]

That, in a nutshell, explains how and why Fawcett got to the Amazon in the first place. It is a point often coyly ignored by cynical modern experts who, while smiling at Fawcett's claims, allow their readers to believe that Fawcett simply went stumbling off into the jungle because of a headful of delusions.

It should be recorded that Fawcett completed his assignment with exemplary accuracy, however, while doing this survey, he claims to have come across some lost cities in the upper reaches of the Amazon Basin in the area of the disputed national boundaries. After completing his official survey work, therefore, Fawcett returned to the Amazon "jungle" to try to find more cities and to discover their significance.

Perhaps the first thing Fawcett did that caused the armchair experts to begin doubting his veracity was to claim that he had shot an anaconda sixty-two feet long "as far as it was possible to measure" because "forty-five feet lay out of the water, and seventeen lay in it."[12] Fawcett had previously recorded that an anaconda of fifty-eight feet in length had been killed in the lower Amazon:

> The manager at Yorongas told me he killed an anaconda fifty-eight feet long in the Lower Amazon. I was inclined to look on this as an exaggeration at the time, but later, as I shall tell, we shot one even larger than that.[12]

Fawcett's claim with respect to the length of anacondas caused him to be regarded as a liar upon his return to civilization. However, as one zoologist familiar with Fawcett's writing has commented:

> Fawcett was certainly a dreamer and his dreams sometimes

led him to cherish the wildest hopes, but he was not a liar . . . one can read through his notebooks from end to end without finding any trace of exaggeration about the size or ferocity of the animals he met with along the Amazon.[14]

One such sober entry by Fawcett is a note he wrote after being attacked by a bushmaster snake (*Lachesis muta*):

It was quite nine feet long and about five inches thick, and the double fangs, if in proportion, would be over an inch in length. Experts claim that these snakes reach a length of fourteen feet, but I have never seen one so big.[15]

Before leaving the subject of the loss of Fawcett's credibility and the length of anacondas, it may be worth noting that an anaconda shot and killed by an official Brazilian expedition to the Chavantes in 1947 was measured and was alleged to have been twenty-three meters in length (seventy-five feet).[16] Many reports and at least two photographs of snakes longer than Fawcett's have come out of the Amazon. Such evidence convinced Lorenz Hagenbeck, director of the Hamburg Zoo, that snakes of a size much larger than allowed by the experts existed in the Amazon Basin.

Fawcett was not necessarily a liar about the size of anacondas, and he is not necessarily a liar about the lost cities he claims to have seen. That is about all that can be said about Fawcett's cities. Their exact location is unknown, except for the fact that Fawcett either first saw them or first heard of them in his work on the border survey. This would place them somewhere on the more southerly eastern slopes of the general "target area."[17]

A more recent adventurer, Pierre Honoré, claims to have found lost cities on those eastern slopes nearer to the part of Colombia and Brazil where the old Muisca culture flourished and from which civilized influences seem to have spread into northern Peru. Honoré claims to have made his discovery in the late 1950s on the upper reaches of the Rio Negro. Without calling Honoré an arrant liar, I must yet confess that the style of his prose makes me a bit suspicious. Writing of his first discovery, of inscribed stones, Honoré tells us:

We had to cut our path yard by yard through the bush and bamboos. In front of us the green wall seemed almost impenetrable. Day after day we fought on toward the stones I was looking for, so the Indians insisted.... After another two hours we reached the bank of a broad river-bed, and there lay the stones I was seeking—in dozens.... I forgot all the hardships I had been through; I forgot hunger and thirst. For hours I stood up to my belly in the mud of the bank and scrutinize the symbols on the stones, line for line, page for page—a great stone picture-book which lay open before me.[18]

According to Honoré, he saw both scripts and drawings, including representations of rhinos, on these stones, and concluded that the material was similar to Cretan and Mycenaen work because of the depiction of horned helmets, cranes in flight, and "godheads with halos."

Later, Honoré claimed to have found a lengthy inscription "typical of the Cretan script," and offers a hand-drawn reproduction in his book. He explains why he could not bring back more tangible evidence of his inscribed stones:

When I found them they were under water, so I could not photograph them. For the river only subsides every ten years, and then the great stone picture-book rises out of the water.[19]

Perhaps.

Pierre Honoré was inspired to mount his expedition to the Rio Negro not only because of Fawcett, but also because of the work of Bernardo da Silva Ramos. Ramos was a most remarkable man. Originally he was one of those Brazilian rubber-prospectors, but where most failed he succeeded in making a fortune. Using the money to educate himself, he became a noted collector of ancient European coins and published a three-volume work on his famous collection. He traveled widely in Egypt, Syria and Greece. Ramos was over fifty when his real life's work began. He returned to his native Amazonia and began to search for the inscribed stones that had been reported from time to time by adventurers, hunters and rubber prospectors. This search lasted twenty-three years, until his death in 1931. He left behind a two-volume work containing over 2,800 inscriptions he had allegedly found in the jungle. In Ramos' opinion, most of these inscriptions had been made by Phoenicians.

Experts have generally maintained that Ramos' collection of inscriptions are either forgeries, natural marks caused by weathering or a combination of both. The Brazilian Ministry of Education announced in 1953: "Brazilian archeology denies altogether the existence of Phoenician inscriptions in any part of the country whatsoever." This seems pretty categorical.

The problem is that some of the marks made by "natural weathering" do happen to be translatable from Phoenician, and it is difficult to understand how the supposed forgeries, some of which are also translatable, could have been accomplished by Ramos. Five decades after Ramos' death, few experts in ancient Phoenician would attempt a forgery, because our knowledge of the language is so uncertain that anyone could make tell-tale mistakes identifiable by trained linguists.[20]

There is no way of knowing whether lost cities and inscribed stones of Old World visitors really exist in the Amazon Basin. We have no irrefutable proof that such things are there, only the assertions of Fawcett, Ramos and Honoré. But it is at least interesting that such evidence is alleged to exist in the very place where it should exist according to the testimony of archeology, geology and the wind and currents coming from the Old World to the New. Yet, in the time of Ramos and Fawcett, these archeological, geological and navigational arguments were not known. The idea of Peruvian culture having been imported from the eastern Andean slopes was a conclusion reached only about 1940. The geological evidence for the oceanic flooding of the Amazon Basin in the recent past is even newer. Honoré, perhaps, could have read about all the good reasons for placing "lost cities" in the upper Basin, but not Ramos or Fawcett.

The experts are skeptical, but they always are. In the last century there was a man who refused to believe that the Homeric stories of the *Odyssey* and *Iliad* were mythical, as all the experts claimed. To him, the detail was too life-like, the world of Troy and Mycenae was drawn too realistically to be fiction. Like Ramos, this man turned to business, made a fortune, and after educating himself in his own way he turned to his life's work. Like Fawcett, Heinrich Schliemann was a dreamer and a romantic. Not only did he have the determination to marry a woman named Helen, but he swore that he would live to adorn his Helen with the jewels of Homer's Helen of Troy. The experts laughed, when they deigned to notice at all.

But Schliemann got the last laugh. With his Homer as a

guide in one hand and a shovel in the other, Schliemann found and excavated both Troy and Mycenae. At Troy he unearthed a hoard of jewels, some of which fitted Homer's description of Helen's jewels, and he photographed his wife, Helen, wearing them. At Mycenae he found a golden death mask that seemed to resemble Homeric descriptions of the king of the Greeks, and he telegraphed an astounded scholarly world: "I have gazed into the face of Agamemnon."

Professional archeologists were quick to flock to the sites of Schliemann's discoveries. They grudgingly admitted that he had found a whole new level of Western civilization and they quickly began the dual process of appropriating the study of it to themselves and denigrating the quality and importance of Schliemann's work. First, the experts justly criticized Schliemann's methods of excavation as being crude and unprofessional, forgetting that without him the lost world of Homer would never have come to light at all. Then, the experts decided that Schliemann had not found the Trojan War and Homeric levels of Mycenae and Troy, but only a later level of occupation. Schliemann had not found the death mask of Agamemnon, but that of some noble who lived a couple of centuries later. As for adorning his wife in ancient gold and photographing her as Helen of Troy, well, Schliemann should have known better. Yes, it was conceded, Schliemann had discovered Mycenae and Troy, but more by sheer luck than knowledgeable research, and he had failed to find the true Homeric levels which had obsessed him. The general consensus was that although the cities of Troy and Mycenae might really have existed, the specific Trojan War and the heroes thereof might well still be mythical. The dreamer Schliemann had certainly not "gazed into the face of Agamemnon."

Perhaps.

It seems that only Arthur Koestler has been able to retain a measure of respect within Western academia while daring to suggest that there are patterns in the great and small events of human life and history that mock the banality of mere coincidence. Koestler has advanced the idea that there seems to be an unconscious direction, purpose and, perhaps, theme to human evolution and discovery that is not perceived adequately by current scientific materialism.[21] The tolerance accorded Koestler by Western intelligensia is itself something of a mystery and can probably be largely attributed to the fact that Koestler is careful to write in acceptably polysyllabic academic jargon, never states his argument baldly, and allows his revolutionary perspective to be inferred. Nonetheless, Koestler's argument cannot be missed. Certainly, some events almost shriek out the demand to conceive of something besides bland coincidence. The circumstances of the Conquest seem to be something of this sort and, I believe, the circumstances of Schliemann's recovery of Mycenaen history is another event in the same category. There is, somehow, a fitness to it all.

So there is probably a good chance that further research will reveal, after all, that Schliemann "gazed into the face of Agamemnon" and that the jewels he found were Helen of Troy's. If this is ever confirmed, one can be certain that the news will not be broken until all those who ridiculed Schliemann, and who make their archeological reputations by correcting and clarifying the crude work he had done, are safely in their reputable graves beyond the reach of the criticism that their pettiness so richly deserves.

But the point of all this is simply that, if lost cities of the Amazon Basin exist, they must prove to be of utmost importance to the understanding of American civilization, and possibly of equal importance to the study of European and African history. Someone must look for them, especially if they have been reported from areas of probable cultural diffusion and by men, like Ramos and Fawcett, who gained nothing and gave much, including their lives, to obtain the knowledge they offered as truth. The cause of science is not served by automatic ridicule of people like Fawcett, Ramos and Schliemann, as the discovery of Schliemann's lost Homeric world shows too well.

Who can say that Fawcett and Ramos did not glimpse another lost chapter of history? One can say, however, that our knowledge has deepened more through the efforts of amateurs like Fawcett, Ramos, Schliemann and Heyerdahl than through the efforts of enfranchised experts.

It is fairly safe to say that various white gods did come to the Americas before Columbus. There may be cities in the upper Amazon Basin, but these cities, when and if they are uncovered, may not necessarily reveal a Phoenician, Cretan, Egyptian or Celtiberian presence only. Some of these lost cities may boast the architecture of black Africans—thick clay-built walls with horn-like cones thrust toward the sky from flat roofs, mysterious and disconcerting profiles to our eyes. At least some of the evidence from botany, archeology and the customs of the Americans should prepare us for this probability, for many hints converge to suggest that black Africans and not white gods helped to mold American civilization on its most profound levels.

11

The Shared Adventure

Perhaps the captain alone awaited what his sovereign would show him.

The King turned the heavy key in a no less robust lock and massive wooden doors studded with nails and reinforced with iron strips creak open.

The captain, not wishing to commit any impropriety, turned away as the interior of the cabinet and its treasures were revealed. His brief glimpse held no glitter of gold or silver or jewels, but merely long and dusty rolls of vellum. Beyond price. As he heard the rustle of the king's hand among the charts, the captain may have gazed out through a tall window to watch the surf break around the barren rocks of Sagres. The murmur of the waves far below may have helped to quell his impatience.

The captain might well have let his thoughts dwell upon Prince Henry, called "the Navigator" though he never went to sea, now a generation and more in his grave. He had started it all, had Henry, here at Sagres, where water stretched away in most directions, for Henry's little fortress had been built at the tip of a lonely promontory. The next land to the west was a New World.

The king may well also have thought of Prince Henry as he viewed the charts and journals of the cabinet, perhaps wondering what had ever possessed his predecessor to begin collecting such things when they never bore their heavy rich fruit in his own time.

There was Fra Mauro's map of Africa made a half-century ago and cracked with age. It was a treasure that had already done its work. It showed a termination to the African continent. Some thought that an Indian captain had sailed past the Cape of Good Hope from the eastward back in 1420—at least so it was rumored—and somehow Fra Mauro had heard of this. He had made his map showing the Cape of Good Hope long

Prince Henry the Navigator

before Diaz had proved for Portugal that it was there.

The king, John II of Portugal, may have looked fondly at this chart, for it was the foundation of his pepper wealth—and of the wealth represented by black humanity. His wealth and that of his kingdom. The king rolled up Fra Mauro's map and put it back in the cabinet.

Ah. There it was! The king grasped the long roll and withdrew it with great care. He turned and began spreading the chart on the large solid table that dominated the center of the room. He may have placed a brass astrolab or wooden compass box on the chart to keep it from curling back upon itself.

How much of it was imaginary? How much of it helpless ignorance, educated guesswork? Fra Mauro had been right. Perhaps Martin de Bohème was as well. There was only one way to find out.

"Don Ferdinand . . ."

"Yes, sire." The captain would have turned quickly, his flashing eyes greedy for the sight of the map.

How many captains had stood like this, awaiting the revelations of a cosmographer's chart, the order of the king? Diego Cão, Bartholomeu Diaz, Vasco da Gama—they had all stood like that in the king's memory.

As they bent together to study the chart, pointed fingers would trace coastlines and cross ocean gaps, heads would shake in careful consideration. Finally, the king would have presented the challenge itself, and the captain would have nodded eagerly in acceptance of the order to undertake the voyage.

The captain would never see Portugal again. He would die in the far reaches of the Pacific, but his ships would return to Europe in triumph.

Such a scene must have occurred, because a member of Magellan's expedition, Pigafetta, wrote:

> The sentiments of every person in the fleet were, that it had no issue in the west; and nothing but the confidence they had in the superior knowledge of the commander could have induced them to prosecute the research. But this great man, as skilful as he was courageous, knew that he was to seek for a passage through an obscure strait: this strait he had seen laid down on a chart of Martin de Bohème, a most excellent cosmographer, which was in the possession of the king of Portugal.[1]

Thus it was that Magellan found the straits at the very tip of South America that today bear his name, and sailed past the barrier of the New World out into the Pacific.

Who had brought knowledge of this "obscure strait" to Europe so that Martin de Bohème could draw it on a chart, so that Magellan could "discover" it and give it his name? Who was the Indian captain who doubled the Cape of Good Hope from the East so that knowledge of Africa's last promontory in the Southern Ocean trickled to Europe, became a fact on Fra Mauro's chart, to be "discovered" by Diaz?

We will never know. Just as we will never know what secret knowledge passed from the mariners of Cape Verde to Perestrello and on to Columbus, so that he could "discover" the New World.

We Westerners have written history in our own image and we have appropriated discoveries to ourselves. But, most discoveries had been made long before by others who remained unnamed.

The Arab cosmographer Abulfeda wrote of voyages around the world—which he knew to be a sphere—as early as 1300 A.D. It is very possible that Abulfeda and a few other geographers of that time knew much about the actual distribution of land and water on the earth. Arabs were in the best position to obtain the most accurate geographical knowledge because of their trading contacts with China, India, West and East Africa and Indonesia.

All of these people, in their turn, voyaged far beyond their own lands. The Chinese once voyaged to a great continent in the far sunrise and could give descriptions of trees and animals there. The West Africans of Mali sent expeditions into the far west. The Indonesians traded out into the Pacific and had some contact with the Polynesians. And we know now that the Polynesians themselves had come from "Tahiti Nui"—Great Tahiti—the continent of America.

Certainly by 1400 A.D. there was no real gap left. There had indeed been "voyages around the world," perhaps not by one ship's company as Abulfeda seems to claim, but by many people on many expeditions: each covered some part of the earth, in a chain of tenuous contact with each other. A careful and diligent Arab cosmographer could piece it all together to make a fairly accurate world map.

This sort of knowledge seems to have trickled into Europe, gradually filling in the huge blanks on European charts, guiding Diaz, Columbus, da Gama, Magellan and all the rest on their voyages of "discovery."

The achievements of the Portuguese and Spanish captains were great and courageous, but they were duplications of no less audacious voyages undertaken by Inca raft, Polynesian double-canoe, Chinese junk, Arab dhow and West African dugout. The knowledge gained on these voyages guided the European caravels on theirs.

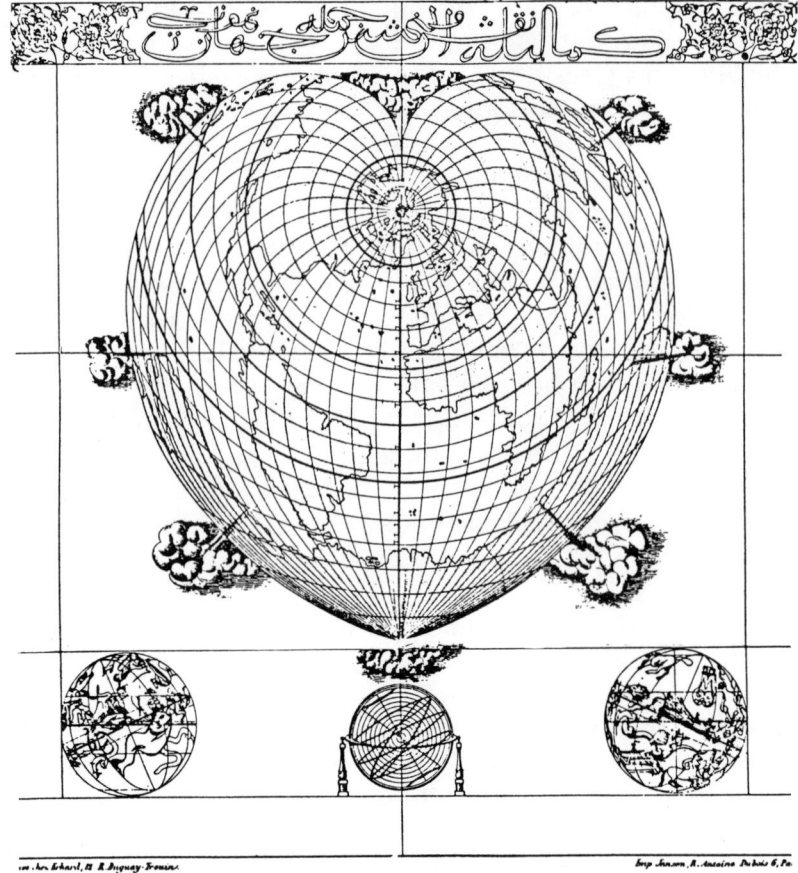

The Hadji Ahmed World Map, 1559

When Diaz and da Gama broke through into the Indian Ocean, they found a flourishing civilization that traded from the mouth of the Zambesi River in Africa to the mouth of the Yellow River in China. The black Africans of medieval Kenya and Tanzania traded in so much Chinese porcelain that archeologists now date many African sites by the kind of Chinese pottery found in them. When da Gama passed by Madagascar, he sailed by an island that had been peopled in the first Christian centuries by Indonesians who had made daring voyages across the entire breadth of the Indian Ocean. It is not surprising that, coming into direct contact with such people, Portuguese map-maker Jorge Reinel was able, as early as 1510, to draw an accurate chart of the Indian Ocean that shows part of the

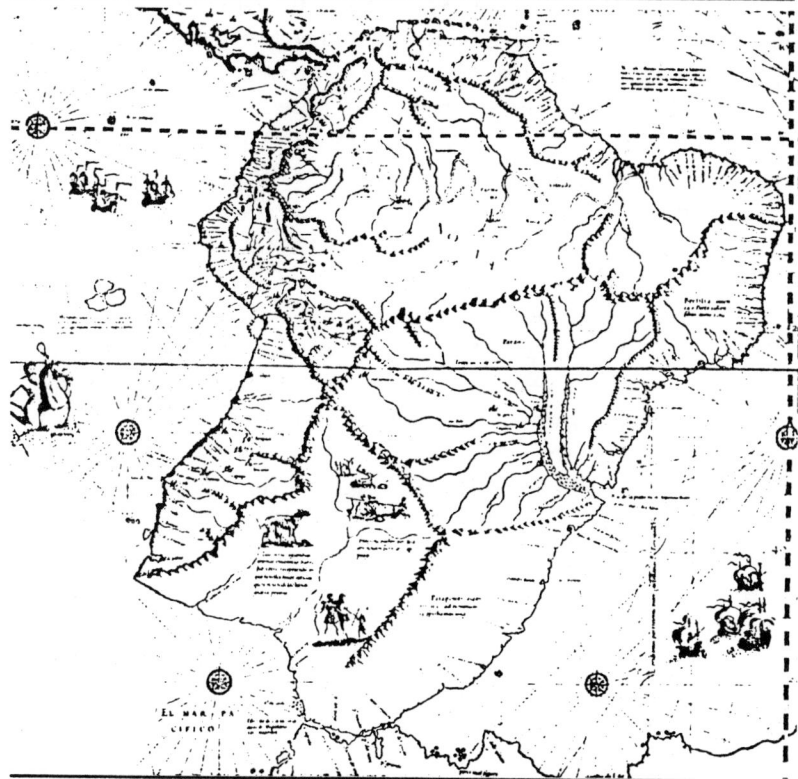

Mercator's Map of South America, 1569

Australian coast, although Australia was supposedly "discovered" 200 years later.

And, as we have seen, it was only from the latitude of Cape Verde that Columbus "concluded for certain" that there was land to the west. Mali mariners had voyaged into the far west only a century before and black Africans from the same area had made many earlier crossings.

When the Spanish arrived in Peru, they followed Inca sailing directions to "discover" islands long known to those American Indians.

What the Europeans "discovered" had long been known by others, and had been charted by Arabs. Arab cartographer Hadji Ahmed was able to draw a world map in 1559 that is astounding in its accuracy. It shows lands and coastlines not "discovered" by Europeans for another two centuries. Although this map was drawn some sixty years after the first voyage of Columbus, there is little doubt that maps of similar accuracy could have been made by Arabs a couple of centuries earlier. Hadji Ahmed did not rely upon European sources; his map shows the outline of the American continents more accurately than the European discoverers were able to draw it. Compare the shape of South America in the Hadji Ahmed map with the shape of South America as conceived by the premier European cartographer Gerhard Mercator ten years later. Obviously Hadji Ahmed did not rely upon the accounts and charts of Portuguese and Spanish voyagers: he had better sources.

The only explanation is that map-makers and geographers like Hadji Ahmed took advantage of the Arab's position as middle-men of the Old World who had contact with peoples at the extreme east and west, from China to West Africa, and who listened to what these people had to say about their voyages. From this information, Hadji Ahmed and others before him managed to piece together the outline of the New World and place islands in the Pacific.

It has been said that the greatest adventure in the human history of our planet was the white man's discovery of the world. But this is only our sort of history and our great distortion of the truth. Diaz, Columbus, da Gama, Medaña, Magellan and all the other heroes of the Age of Discovery were guided by the knowledge of men of all races.

Black Africans participated in this adventure. Their mariners sailed across the Atlantic both in very early and medieval times, for so it is written in both the archeological record of the New World and books of North African Arabs. Black Africans participated no less than Vikings, Portuguese, Spaniards, Chinese, Polynesians or Arabs in the discovery of the world.

It was a shared adventure, and this book is my reconstruction of an unrecorded and unrecognized black African contribution to our common human achievement.

Notes

Chapter One
1. Ferdinand Colón, *Life of Admiral Christopher Columbus*, trans. B. Keen (London: Greenwood Press, 1978), p. 118.
2. *Ibid.*, p. 123.
3. Frederick J. Pohl, *The Lost Discovery* (New York: W. W. Norton & Company Inc., 1952), p. 242.
4. Colón, *op. cit.*
5. Records of these voyages are contained in Icelandic sagas, particularly *Eriks Saga Rauda* ("Eric the Red's Saga"), the *Landnamabok* (the "Taking of the Land Book"), the *Flateyjarbok* (the "Flat Island Book"), the *Hauksbok* ("Hauk's Book") and ecclesiastical records. The sagas also preserve hints that voyages to the New World took place before Lief Ericsson's voyage of about 1000 A.D. The *Landnamabok* relates that one Ari Marson sailed to the New World in 983, driven there by storms, and was baptized in "White Man's Land" also called Great Ireland (Irland ad Mikla) by the Norse. Other sagas state that "White Man's Land" was inland from Vinland. It is unclear who could have baptized Ari Marson in the New World if not Irish priests who, according to both Norse sagas and Irish tradition preserved in the Brendan tales (*Navigatio Sancti Brendani Abbatis*), crossed the Atlantic as early as the fifth century A.D.
6. Pohl, *op. cit.*, p. 204.
7. Christopher Columbus, *Journals and Letters* (London: Hakluyt Society, 1971).
8. *Ibid.*
9. *Ibid.*
10. See description of the Neo-boreal climate by Dr. J. E. Katzenback of the University of Wisconsin in *The Weather Conspiracy* (New York: Ballantine, 1977). See also CIA report designated "Office of Political Research—401" (1974), which analyzes the effect of climatic change in past historical times, including the medieval period, and in contemporary times.
11. Colón, *op. cit.*, p. 118.
12. al-Omari, Ibn Fadl Allah, *Masalik al Absar fi Mamalik al Absar*, Cairo, c. 1942 (Paris. Gaudefroy-Demembynes, 1927) French translation. The English translation here is from Basil Davidson's *The Lost Cities of Africa* (Boston: Little, Brown and Company, 1959), which compares well with hitherto unpublished accounts of the same Atlantic voyage supplied to me by Dr. J. B. Webster, Professor of African History at Dalhousie University. *See Lost Cities of Africa*, pp. 74-75.
13. Pohl, *op. cit.*, p. 239.
14. Strangely enough, traditional vessels and modern yachts average about the same speed on ocean crossings, about 70-100 miles per day. See Sir Francis

Chichester's *Along the Clipper Way* for a discussion of average duration of ocean passages.
15. Pohl, *op. cit.*, p. 247.
16. Elizabeth Miller, "The Science of Columbus," *Indiana Historical Society*, vol. 7, 1923, pp. 449-80.
17. Pohl, *op. cit.*, p. 250.
18. Columbus, *op. cit.*
19. al-Omari, *op. cit.*, ch. 10.
20. See Tim Severin's *The Brendan Voyage* (London: Hutchinson, 1978) for a complete account of the traditional Brendan cycle of alleged Atlantic voyages and of Severin's replica voyage in a leather boat from Ireland to Newfoundland. One of the most interesting aspects of Severin's experience was the inefficiency of modern materials and foods when compared with medieval materials and foods. Although Severin originally had no intention of relying upon medieval materials and rations except in the wood and leather construction of the *Brendan* replica boat itself, he and his crew found during the first season of sailing that modern tools and clothing proved inadequate, and that modern "survival rations" were unappetizing. For the second season of sailing, from Iceland to North America, Brendan's crew relied upon medieval clothing, tools and diet with much satisfaction. Similarly, Heyerdahl's crew aboard *Ra I* and *Ra II* ate ancient Egyptian and Berber foods, preserved according to ancient and traditional methods, and considered themselves very well fed. The conclusion of both Severin and Heyerdahl was that the "primitive" sailor was in many ways better equipped for oceanic voyaging than his modern yachting counterpart.
21. Davidson, *Lost Cities*, p. 131.
22. *Ibid.*
23. Ibn Battuta (Mohammed Ibn Allah), *Travels in Asia and Africa*, trans. H. A. R. Gibb (1929) (Morocco, 1356). See also *Lost Cities*, p. 79.
24. R. H. Bacon, *Benin, the City of Blood* (London, 1897). See also *Lost Cities*, p. 134.
25. Davidson, *Lost Cities*, p. 198.
26. For this quote and the following ones by David Hume and Sir Arthur Kirby, see both Davidson, *Lost Cities*, pp. 130-38, and Ashley Montagu's *Man's Most Dangerous Myth: The Fallacy of Race* (New York: Oxford University Press, 1974), pp. 14-124, for many more opinions of the same ilk.
27. Claude Levi-Strauss, *Tristes Tropiques* (New York: Atheneum, 1974), p. 109.
28. Montagu, *op. cit.*, p. 96.
29. Hannah Arendt, *On Violence* (New York: Harcourt, Brace & World, 1969) and Michael Bradley, *The Iceman Inheritance* (Toronto: Dorset Publishing, Inc., 1978) both make the point that Western history is both quantitatively and qualitatively more violent than the histories of other peoples.

Chapter Two

1. Carleton S. Coon, *The Origin of Races* (New York: Alfred A. Knopf, 1962), pp. 588-656.
2. Davidson, *Lost Cities*, p. 7.
3. *Ibid.* See also *A History of West Africa* (Garden City: Doubleday, 1966), by the same author with F. K. Buah.
4. *Lost Cities.*, p. 7.

5. Henri Lhote, *A la Découverte des Fresques du Tassili*, 1958.
6. Davidson, *Lost Cities*, p. 60.
7. *Ibid.*, p. 63.
8. Robert Graves, *The White Goddess* (London: Faber and Faber, 1961). Graves gives many other examples of mythological parallels between tropical Africa and the Mediterranean, and notes that Sir Flinders Petrie postulates a "sacred league between Libya and the Greek mainland well back into the third millenium B.C." The link between Mediterranean and tropical West African mythology and religion must have been a common, and very ancient, culture source in the Sahara. See pp. 61-73, and particularly p. 489.
9. Barry Fell, *America B.C.* (New York: Simon & Schuster, 1976).
10. Davidson, *Lost Cities*, p. 61. See also *A History of West Africa*.
11. Graves, *op. cit.*, pp. 81-84.
12. Davidson, *Lost Cities*, pp. 59-70.
13. Graves, *op. cit.*, p. 45.
14. Davidson, *Lost Cities*, p. 59, and *A History of West Africa*, pp. 16-17, 97-98. See also B. E. B. Fagg, "A Life-sized Terracotta Head from Nok," *Man*, 1956.
15. Davidson quoting Sayce in *A History of West Africa*, p. 2; G. A. Wainwright, "Iron in the Napatan and Meroitic Ages," *Sudan Notes and Records*, 1945.
16. See Davidson, *Lost Cities*, pp. 64-107, and *A History of West Africa* for English translations of early Arabic sources.
17. Davidson, *Lost Cities*, for Arabic sources relating to West African cities and military power. Also Paul Herrmann, *Conquest by Man* (London: Hamish Hamilton, 1954) for similar material and some Roman sources.
18. Ibn Battuta, *op. cit.* See also Herrmann, *op. cit.* for a brief biography of Battuta and an account of his travels. See Davidson, *Lost Cities*, pp. 93-95.
19. Herodotus, *The Histories* (New York: Dutton, 1964), vol. 2, p. 267.
20. See Colin Renfrew, *Before Civilization* (London: Jonathan Cape, 1973), pp. 6-35 for a complete account of the radio carbon calibration revolution in ancient archeology. It is now known that the megaliths of Western Europe are older than the pyramids of Egypt.
21. Basil Davidson, *The African Genius* (Boston: Little, Brown and Company, 1969), p. 53.
22. M. J. Herskovits, *The Human Factor in Changing Africa* (London: Routledge, 1962).

Chapter Three

1. Thor Heyerdahl, *The Ra Expedition* (New York: Doubleday, 1971), p. 13.
2. Immanuel Velikovsky, *The Peoples of the Sea* (New York: Doubleday, 1971), p. 205. Velikovsky quoting O.G.S. Crawford.
3. *Ibid.*, p. 211.
4. *Ibid.*, p. 208.
5. *Ibid.*, p. xvi. In *The Peoples of the Sea*, Velikovsky gives a detailed account of the development of Egyptian chronology as it has been presently constructed and offers an equally detailed discussion of his reasons for disputing the accuracy of this chronology. See also Renfrew's *Before Civilization* for a lucid discussion of the inaccuracy of Carbon 14 dates prior to about 1200 B.C. and the necessity of calibrating such early dates with dendrochronology (a chronology based upon the annual growth rings of trees) and varve counts.

("Varves" are successive lines of glacial retreat.) Something happened about 1200 B.C. that increased the hydrocarbon content of the environment. Velikovsky relates this to a worldwide catastrophe caused by the close approach of Venus to Earth about that time, while conventional experts maintain that the gigantic eruption of the Santorini volcano in the Mediterranean might have been sufficient to produce a worldwide increase in hydrocarbons. Velikovsky, however, believes that Santorini and other volcanoes erupted because of the tectonic pressures resulting from the close approach of Venus. It is now known that tectonic activity on earth is affected by the phases of the moon as well as by the relative positions of the other planets. See *The Jupiter Effect* by John Gribben and Stephen Plagemann (New York: Walker and Co., 1974) for an analysis of the complicated earth-planetary interplay of gravitational forces.

Chapter Four

1. Matthew W. Stirling, "La Venta Man," *Indians of the Americas* (Washington: National Geographic Society, 1958), p. 219.
2. *Ibid.*, p. 221.
3. *Ibid.*, p. 232.
4. *Ibid.*
5. *Ibid.*, p. 233.
6. See H. D. Disselhoff and Sigvald Linné, *Art of the World: Ancient America* (London: Methuen, 1961), p. 20, where it is stated that Disselhoff and Krickeberg "discovered a startling affinity between the pottery at Tlatico and that of the pan-Peruvian Chavin culture in regard to the shape of some vessels and their decoration. This has been established by Dr. Disselhoff after many years of study, during the course of which he has carried out a number of excavations."
7. That the Kushite lion-man god, if transplanted to West Africa, would logically become a leopard-man makes some sense because there are no lions in the forested parts of West Africa, where the leopard is the largest feline predator. Mysterious "leopard societies" exist in West Africa today. However, if this Kushite lion-man complex was carried to West Africa in early times, there may have been some reluctance to abandon the lion template altogether; and, while there are no true lions in the forests of West Africa, there is the smaller "golden cat" (*Profelis aurata*), which is more lionlike than the leopard. It seems that some of the ancient Kushite lion-man attributes were transferred to both the leopard and the golden cat to establish "religious" or "magic" or "ju-ju" cults around both animals.
8. Matthew W. Stirling, "Discovering the New World's Oldest Dated Work of Man."
9. The quetzal bird is Guatemala's national symbol and appears on stamps, coins and the nation's coat of arms. It is also an endangered species, according to a recent news item on the Canadian Broadcasting Corporation's public affairs radio program "As It Happens."

Chapter Five

1. Ivan T. Sanderson, *Abominable Snowmen: legend come to life, the story*

of subhumans on five continents from the early ice age until today (Radnor: Chilton Book Company, 1961). Although this book is primarily about hominids, it is a vast compendium of geographic and phytozoological research regarding environmental changes that occurred during the past 100,000 years.
2. *Ibid.*, p. 156.
3. *Ibid.*, p. 155.
4. *Ibid.*, p. 176. See also zoologist Gerald Durrell's *Two Tickets to Adventure* for an entertaining description of the flora and fauna of these sand dunes.
5. Disselhoff and Linné, *op. cit.*, pp. 137-53.
6. *Ibid.*, See p. 143 particularly.
7. *Ibid.*, p. 239.
8. *Ibid.*, pp. 238-47.
9. Both British adventurer Percy Fawcett and American anthropologist A. H. Verrill describe this process in uncertain terms, but neither identifies the plant. Fawcett and Verrill also refer to another unidentified plant, the juices of which can dissolve both stone and metal very rapidly. Reports such as these fuel persistent speculation that much South American precision stonework was accomplished with a vegetable paste that etched through massive blocks quickly, allowing great control by skilled masons. Certainly, it is something of a mystery how some of the Inca stonework was accomplished with the tools we know them to have possessed.
10. Disselhoff and Linné, *op. cit.*, p. 163.
11. Philip Ainsworth Means, "The Incas: Empire Builders of the Andes," *Indians of the Americas*, pp. 312-13.

Chapter Six

1. Charles Borden, *Sea Quest* (Philadelphia: Macrae, 1966). Borden gives an account of Atlantic crossings in a number of unlikely craft, as does Chichester in *Along the Clipper Way*.
2. Pereira Pacheco, *Esmeraldo*, pp. 136-37, 146-47.
3. P. de Marees, *A Description and Historical Declaration of the Gold Kingdom of Guinea*. English translation in *Purchas His Pilgrims* (Glasgow, 1905), vol. VI, pp. 247-366.
4. Lionel Casson, *Ships and Seamanship in the Ancient World* (Princeton: Princeton University Press, 1971), pp. 243-44.
5. Bjorn Landström, *Ships of the Pharaohs* (New York: Doubleday, 1970), p. 11.
6. Philip Ainsworth Means, "Pre-Spanish Navigation Off the Andean Coast," *American Neptune*, vol. II, no. 2, 1942.
7. Thor Heyerdahl, *American Indians in the Pacific*. See also Heyerdahl's *Sea Routes to Polynesia*, *The Ra Expedition*, and *Kon Tiki* for discussions of Peruvian navigation.
8. Juan de Sáamanos, *Relacion de los premeros descubrimientos de Francisco Pizarro, etc.* (Madrid, 1844) n.p.
9. Pascual de Andagoya, Hakluyt Society, vol. XXXIV, 1865.
10. Bernabé Cobo, *Historio del Nuevo Mondo* (Seville, 1890).
11. Thor Heyerdahl, *Sea Routes to Polynesia* (London: George Allen and Unwin, 1968), p. 107.
12. *Ibid.*, p. 109.

Chapter Seven

1. Thor Heyerdahl, *The Ra Expedition*, p. 5.
2. Landström, *op. cit.*, pp. 20-21.

Chapter Eight

1. E. Nordenskiold, "Origin of the Indian Civilizations in South America," *Comp. Ethnogr. Stud.*, vol. LX, Gothenburg, p. 269.
2. C. O. Sauer, "Cultivated Plants of South and Central America," Steward, 1950, p. 506.
3. J. B. Hutchinson, R. A. Silow and S. G. Stephens, *The Evolution of the Gossypium and the Differentiation of the Cultivated Cottons*, 1947, pp. 74-98.
4. Heyerdahl, *American Indians*, p. 447.
5. *Ibid.*, p. 451.
6. Hutchinson et al., *The Evolution of Gossypium*, pp. 65-73.
7. Heyerdahl, *American Indians*, p. 481.
8. See W. H. Prescott's *History of the Conquest of Peru*, p. 147; A. Rochebrun's *Recherches d'ethnographie botanique sur la flore des sépultures peruviennes d'Ancon*, pp. 346 and 348; and M. Wittmack's *Die Nutzpflantzen der alter Peruaner*, p. 340 for evidence of plantain in pre-Spanish graves. See also vol. V of the *Handbook of South American Indians*, p. 744, where the groundnut (peanut) of West Africa is listed as a plant domesticated in South America before Columbus.

Chapter Nine

1. All material on the length of anacondas, and on the length and coloration of pythons has been drawn from Dr. Bernard Heuvelmans' *On the Track of Unknown Animals* (London: Rupert Hart-Davies, 1958). This book, like Sanderson's *Abominable Snowmen*, contains a wealth of geographical, ethnographic and even historical information.
2. *Ibid.*
3. *Ibid.*

Chapter Ten

1. Paul Herrmann, *Conquest by Man* (New York: Harper & Brothers, 1954), p. 184. Also see pp. 167-204.
2. *Ibid.*, p. 167.
3. *Ibid.*, p. 165.
4. *Ibid.*, p. 171.
5. Walter Krickeberg, *Märchen des Azteken, Maya und Muiska* (Jena, 1928). See also *Beiträge zur Frage der alten kulturgeschichtlichen Bezeihungen zwischen Nord- und Südamerika* (1934), Berlin: *Ztschr. f. Ethn.*, vol. LXVI.
6. From Herrmann, *Conquest*, p. 187. See also Heyerdahl, *Kon Tiki*, and Krickeberg, where the Bochica legend is discussed.
7. Thor Heyerdahl, *Aku Aku* (London: George Allen and Unwin, 1958).
8. Inca Garcilasso de la Vega, *Premera Parte de los Comentarios Reales que*

tratan del origen de los Incas, Etc. (English translation by Hakluyt Society, vols. XLI-XLV, London, 1871).
9. Pedro Pizarro, *Relation of the Discovery and Conquest of the Kingdoms of Peru*, tr. P. A. Means (New York, 1921).
10. Herrmann, *op. cit.*, p. 184.
11. Heuvelmans, *op. cit.*, p. 169.
12. Percy Fawcett, *Exploration Fawcett* (Glasgow: Blackie and Son, 1972), p. 84.
13. *Ibid.*, p. 89.
14. Heuvelmans, *op. cit.*, p. 170.
15. Fawcett, *op. cit.*, p. 103.
16. Heuvelmans, *op. cit.*, pp. 68-85.
17. *Exploration Fawcett* makes fascinating reading. Major Fawcett organized several expeditions to South America, and he tended to concentrate his search on the eastern slopes of the Andes in the area of Bolivia. He never related the exact location of the cities he had seen, but he describes a couple of cities in detail insofar as the ruins were not covered by vegetation. My own opinion is that *Exploration Fawcett* is convincingly written.
18. Pierre Honoré, *In Quest of the White God* (New York, 1963), p. 235.
19. *Ibid.*, p. 238.
20. There is a more contemporary controversy of the same sort. Professors Barry Fell of Harvard and George Carter of Texas A. and M. claim to have found and deciphered Celtiberian (Celtic Iberian/Cartheginian/Phoenician) inscriptions in New England and elsewhere in North America. The most northerly inscription is allegedly in Sherbrooke, Quebec. It was the basis for a Canadian Broadcasting Corporation radio program ("Ideas") in 1977. Fell and Carter also claim to have discovered traces of Libyan, Egyptian and Greek writing in North America. See *America B.C.* and *Saga America* for the presentation of this evidence, which has not, however, convinced all the experts.
21. Arthur Koestler's *The Ghost in the Machine*, *The Sleepwalkers* and *The Roots of Coincidence*.

Chapter Eleven

1. F. Pigafetta, *A Report on the Kingdom of Congo, Etc.* (London, 1881).

Index

Abulfeda, 5, 179
Ahmed, Hadji, 181-182
Akan, death mask, 143
Andagoya, P. de, 111
Andean mariners, achievements of, 110
Atahualpa, 39, 90, 166
Aymara Indians, 132
Aztecs, 39, 49, 50, 52, 53, 56, 63, 64, 150, 157, 158, 159, 166, 167
and Spanish Conquest, 157

Bantu culture, and spiritual attributes of snakes, 151-152
Black Caribs, 141
Blaxland, George, 112
Blom, Frans, 56
Blyth, Chay, 99, 109
Bochica (Sua, Xue), 162, 165
Bohème, Martin de, 178
Book of Ballymote, 21
bottle gourd (calabash: *Lagenaria siceraria*), 11, 85, 88, 135-6, 137, 138, 141
Buck, Peter, 112, 135

Caamaño, Jijón y, 141
Cacique of Cintla, 158
Candia, Pedro de, 162
carbon-dating, 46
Carter, G.F., 136
Chancas, 164
Chavero, Alfredo, 54
Chavin culture, 43, 57, 68, 82, 84 85, 86, 87, 88, 89, 129, 137
influence on pan-Mexican culture complex, 57, 68
Chibchan languages, 141, 162
Chimu, 89
Chinese, expeditions to North America of, 37-38
Cobo, Bernabé, 111
Columbus, Christopher, 1-14, 37, 38, 39, 43, 50, 98, 118, 138, 139, 156, 174, 179, 180, 181, 182
Coon, Carleton, 19
Cortéz, Hernando, 49-50, 51, 52, 53, 68, 157-159, 166, 167
Cotton, West African cultivation of, 136-138, 141

Da Gama, Vasco, 16, 95, 178, 179, 180, 182
Davidson, Anne, 93, 97
Davidson, Basil, 2, 16, 32, 36-37, 91, 141, 145
Diaz, Bartholomeu, 1, 2, 177, 178, 179, 180, 182
Disselhoff, H.D., 51, 68, 77, 79, 86

ear-lengthening, 84, 89, 145-146, 154
El Dorado, 80, 88, 89, 168
El Fazari, 28-29
El Mas'udi, 32
El Zouhi, 29
Ericsson, Lief, 97, 118
Estrada, Emilio, 116

Fawcett, Percy, 168-170, 171, 172, 174

Graves, Robert, 21
guara boards, 51, 105-106, 113-118, 132

Hagenbeck, Lorenz, 170
Hall, H.R., 45
Hatshepsut, 107
Hatun Tupac, 163-164
Herodotus, 27, 33
Herrmann, Paul, 158, 167
Herskovits, M.J., 91, 141
Heyerdahl, Thor, 18, 40-41, 64, 66, 92, 93, 106, 109, 110, 111, 113, 114, 116-119, 120, 134, 136, 139, 140, 145-156, 163, 168, 174
Hittite empire, 46
Honoré, Pierre, 55, 156, 170-171, 172
Hornaday, William, 150
Hoyle, Larco, 84
Huaxtecs, 49, 50, 52, 54
Huayna Capac, 166
Hume, David, 17
Hutchinson, T.J., 112

Ibn Amir Hajib, 11
Ibn Battuta, 15, 31
Incas, 18, 39, 49, 79, 80, 88, 89, 90, 91, 92, 105, 110, 111, 112, 116, 117, 129, 130, 132, 134, 145, 157, 162-164, 166, 167, 181
  and ear-lengthening, 89, 145
  and guara navigation, 18, 105, 132
  in Polynesia, 38, 112
  sea-going accomplishments of, 38, 111, 130
  and Spanish Conquest, 157
  sun worship of, 88-89
Irish, expeditions to the Americas of, 9, 13, 14, 37, 38, 156
  leather boats of, 14, 92, 97
  legends of "Iargalon", 14
Ixtlilxochitl, 159

Jukas, 141

Kanem-Bornu, empire of, 30
Kankan Musa, 5, 6, 7, 11, 12, 95, 98, 109
Karlsefni, Thorfinn, 134
Kirby, Sir Arthur, 17
Koestler, Arthur, 173-174
Krickeberg, Walter, 51, 161
Kukulcan, see Quetzalcoatl
Kush, kingdom of, 27-28, 32, 58, 59-60, 148, 150, 151, 153, 154
  lion-headed gods of, 58-60, 154
  migrations to South America of, 154
  serpent as religious symbol of, 148, 150

Lagenaria, see bottle gourd
Landström, Björn, 120, 123, 128
Lhote, Henri, 20, 32, 137
Linné, Siguald, 86
Lizarraga, Reginaldo de, 111
'long-ears' civilization, of Easter Island, 164
Lothrop, S.K., 111

Magellan, Ferñao de Magalhaes, 178, 179, 182
Malentzin (Doña Marina), 158-159, 161
Mali, empire of, 5, 10, 11,15, 16, 30, 34, 35
  mariners of, 6, 7, 11, 13
  metal-working of, 34
  ships of, 95
Manco Capac, 90
Mandinga, 12, 128, 141
Manetho, 45
Marees, Pieter de, 97, 98
Marina, Doña, see Malentzin
Masalık-al-absad, 5, 11
matrilinear succession, 28, 31, 89
Mauro, Fran, 176, 177, 178, 179
Mayas, 49, 50, 51, 53, 54, 56, 57, 60-64, 67-68, 75, 86, 147, 150, 154, 158, 159, 162

calendar of, 56, 62, 154
hieroglyphic writing system of, 62
New Empire of, 53, 154
Old Empire of, 61, 67
and serpent as religious symbol, 147, 150
Temple of warriors of, 64-67, 155
"Wotan" legend of, 161, 165
Mayer, Charles, 150
Means, Philip Ainsworth, 90
Mendaña, Alvaro de, 182
Mercator, Gerhard, 182
Meroë excavation, 27
Miller, Elizabeth, 8
Mixtecs, 49, 50, 52, 54, 57
Moche culture, 85-86, 87, 88, 89
Montejo, Francisco de, 53
Montezuma, 39, 49, 50, 158-159, 162, 167
Moorish-Spanish war, 15
Muisa culture, 69, 72, 80, 87, 129, 143, 170
multiple-leg pottery, 144

Nauer people, the, 151
Nazcas, 89
Nok culture, 26-27, 33
Nompanem, 162, 165
Nordenskiold, E., 135
Norse, explorations of, 3, 9, 13, 37, 38, 97, 156, 161-162
naval architecture of, 97, 100-102
Nubian rock drawings, 23, 104-105, 108, 109, 120, 122, 123-124, 125, 127, 132

Olmecs, 49, 50, 53, 54, 56-60, 61, 62, 67, 86, 129
Orellana, F. de, 138

Park, Mungo, 31
Pereira, Pacheco, 97, 98
Perestrello, 1, 2, 5-6, 7, 179
Petrie, Sir Flinders, 120
Pizarro, Francisco, 111, 145, 157, 162, 166, 167

Pizarro, Pedro, 167
plantain, 135, 138-139, 141
Pohl, Frederick, 2, 6, 7, 8
pyramids, 41, 42, 44, 86

Quetzalcoatl, 59, 62, 63, 64, 68, 84, 86, 146-150, 152-155, 158, 160-162, 165

ram, as religious symbol, 23-25
Ramos, Bernardo da Silva, 171-172, 174
Reinel, Jorge, 180
relics, African, in the new world, 11, 13
Ridgway, John, 99, 109
Roggeveen, Jacob, 112
roof combs, in African architecture, 87
in the "New World", 86-88

Sáamanos, Juan de, 111
Saharan culture, ancient, 21-22, 24-25, 26
St. Brendan, 14
Sanderson, Ivan T., 70, 71
Sauer, C.O., 136, 139
Schliemann, Henrich, 172-173, 174
serpent, as religious symbol, 23-24, 86, 146-153
Severin, Tim, 14, 92, 97
ship construction, European, 99-102
Sinchi Rocha, 88-89, 90
slavery, 2, 5, 6, 15, 16, 19, 31-32, 37, 141
Sobo, 130
Spanish Conquest, 111, 113, 157-159, 166-167, 174
Stevenson, W. B., 111
Stirling, Matthew, 54, 56-57

Tairona, 80
Tiahuanaco, 89, 164-165
Toltecs, 49, 50, 52, 53, 56, 62, 63, 64, 68, 154, 162
Torquemada, Juan de, 160, 161

Tunka Manin, 30
Tutankhamen, 46

Velasco, Pedro de, 4
Velikovsky, Immanuel, 45-47
Villiers, Alan, 95
viracocha, 162-167
von Chamisse, Adalbert, 111
Voss, J.C., 94

Weiant, C.W., 54
Wene, 37
West African vessels, 93-99, 109, 110,
    119, 124, 125, 127-133, 140
windward sailing, 103-109

Yahuar Huaccac, 164

Zapotecs, 49, 50, 52, 54, 56, 57